Anonymous

Echoes from the Gun of 1861 - A Book for Boys

No. 3

Anonymous

Echoes from the Gun of 1861 - A Book for Boys
No. 3

ISBN/EAN: 9783337064891

Printed in Europe, USA, Canada, Australia, Japan

Cover: Foto ©Andreas Hilbeck / pixelio.de

More available books at **www.hansebooks.com**

SUNSET STORIES.

ECHOES FROM THE GUN OF 1861.

A BOOK FOR BOYS.

No. 3.

"In the world's broad field of battle,
In the bivouac of life,
Be not like dumb driven cattle!
Be a hero in the strife!"

LORING, Publisher,
319 WASHINGTON STREET,
BOSTON.
1864.

Entered according to Act of Congress, in the year 1864, by
A. K. LORING,
In the Clerk's Office of the District Court of the District of Massachusetts.

Stereotyped and Printed by
J. E. FARWELL AND COMPANY,
37 Congress Street Boston.

CONTENTS.

CHAPTER		PAGE
I.	Three Brothers	13
II.	Circumstances	19
III.	Thornton Aroused at Last	24
IV.	Wishes and Plans	31
V.	Drilling and Waiting	41
VI.	Battle and Defeat	49
VII.	After the Battle	59
VIII.	Horace posts his Pickets	68
IX.	Horace gains the Victory	77
X.	Thornton learns by Experience the Truth of an old Proverb	87
XI.	Insidious Foes	100
XII.	The Spider and the Fly	115
XIII.	Thornton's Adventure, and Lee's Romance	124
XIV.	Horace is taken Prisoner	140
XV.	Bitter Fruits	150

CONTENTS.

CHAPTER		PAGE
XVI.	VAN WINS THE PRIZE	157
XVII.	TRUTH PREVAILS	163
XVIII.	HORACE MANIFESTS AN UNFAILING SIGN OF CONVALESCENCE	179
XIX.	"LIGHTS AND SHADOWS"	188
XX.	"POOR NED," AND THE BABES IN THE WOOD	198
XXI.	GETTYSBURG AND THE HOSPITAL	211
XXII.	MR. GREY'S LIBRARY ONCE MORE	222
XXIII.	PROMOTION	232
XXIV.	HORACE GAINS ANOTHER VICTORY	240

INTRODUCTION.

There was no "lull" in the sunset circle of listeners when grandma finished reading "Sketches of Doll Life." What the young critics said will not interest boys, probably, with the exception of Harry's and Walter's comments, which I give you.

"They are very well for babies' and little girls' stories, I dare say," said Harry, patronizingly; "but you can't expect boys to care about dolls, though I like the part about Frank well enough."

"I did n't listen much," said Walter. "I hope it is our turn now, grandma, and that you'll give us a jolly soldier story, all about camp life, and fighting, and scrapes, and everything."

"Yes," said grandma, taking out quite a formidable-looking manuscript; "I have written your soldier story, not altogether about soldiers in camp and on the battle-field, but in part about younger soldiers, of whom there are now so many thousands at home, drilling in school, and in play, and at all times and seasons, in fact, when they are awake, for future active service. They fight battles, too; are defeated and disheartened, or are victorious and encouraged. These drills and battles are not known over the land by bulletins and through newspapers; but they are many of them as severe and as grand battles as ever were fought; their reward is greater than the hero's glory, and their record is on high."

"I know what grandma means," whispered Harry to Walter, — "she means the battles we fight with ourselves; but I don't see how we are drilling all the time, or who our drill-master is."

"Hush!" said Walter; "the story will explain that, perhaps."

"As a rule," continued grandma, "I have not undertaken to give localities or dates, — though both are sometimes mentioned, — because the purpose of my story did not require it, and because you can get facts of that sort much better from those who have been eye-witnesses and participators in what they relate.

"After reading the vividly portrayed realities of such grand books as Hosmer's 'Color Guard,' or Carleton's 'Days and Nights on the Battle-Field,' I could hardly venture to sit down in my quiet room, and undertake to give you an account of that which I had never seen. But the incidents I have given are all of them facts, or founded upon facts, and as such must have an interest and value to you. My story commences with an appeal to the Boys of *Our Country.*"

"But, grandma," said Walter, "boys'll skip it, at least till they get through the book, and have found out what the story is."

"Never mind," answered grandma; "it will answer my purpose just as well if they read it at the close as the beginning of the book. As for you," she added, laughing, "you must hear it whether you will or no, as I have you in my power. So attention all, and listen to me."

AN APPEAL

TO THE

BOYS OF OUR COUNTRY.

My young friends, boys of twelve years of age and upwards, do you know what it is to have a country, — to live for it, to add your mite of effort towards its salvation, in this its hour of peril?

Do you know what it is to long to be a man, that you may fight, and, if need be, die for your country?

Do you know what it is to have your cheeks flush and your hearts glow with loyal zeal as you look upon the beautiful star-spangled banner, fighting for love of which many a brave heart, young in years, but old in valor, has given up its last drop of blood?

Ah, yes! I know you do. I have seen it in your earnest, honest faces; I have heard it in words of patriotism that burst frank and indignant from your lips. I know many of you shuddered as you read, but a short time since, in one of our leading periodicals, that thrilling story, entitled, "A Man without a Country." You pitied that man from the depths of your generous boy nature, and you felt almost indignant when you found the story was fiction, not fact. You could hardly believe fiction could seem so real, and you thought it was cruel to arouse your sympathies so needlessly. But it was not cruel, nor needless. The writer of that story, a true lover of his country, knew that fiction would reach where grave argument would not. Perhaps the story was not written for boys; but no matter, — it has a lesson for you as for others, and I think all of you who have read it feel more deeply than before the priceless blessing of having a country.

Yes, *you* are boys with a country, — and what a country! Your geographies tell you of its varied climate, producing the fruits of almost every zone; its diversified surface; its grand mountains and peaceful valleys; its ice-bound wastes, and its broad prairies; its majestic rivers and inland seas; of its vast resources, its wealth of mines, and agricultural products. A country to which Nature has been so bountiful that she has given freely of the sweet and the fatness considered in Eastern lands so essential to luxury; for her trees and brakes yield sugar, and out of her secret storehouses bubble wells of oil.

A country so abounding in wealth and resources that it has astonished the civilized world on the other side of the ocean by carrying on its own wars. A country whose past history is so glorious, and whose prosperity has been so unexampled, as almost to make us forget that not of our own might and power have we done all this. A country whose Government is so great a blessing to all, that Rebellion against it has aroused almost a whole nation as one man.

And this is the land each of you can say is *my* country. And if you say the words and feel them in the depth and breadth of their meaning, you are now fitting yourselves to be true patriots, — not Benedict Arnolds, but Washingtons; and you will not be partisans, or politicians, but you will be lovers of your country; and you will feel that this is a war not of North and South, of Lincoln and Davis, but a war of right and wrong, and hence God's war.

And if it is the wish and settled purpose of your heart, as I know it is with some of you, to engage in this war, if your services are needed, when you are old enough to do so, you must remember that now is your best time to drill for it. I do not refer only to the drill most of you get in the military companies which you have formed for your amusement, — though this sort of drilling will be of great service to you, — but I refer to the moral drill you must all pass through to enable you to become true soldiers, where your drill-master is the Eternal principle of truth and right, who makes known his behests to you through the voice of conscience. Obedience to this voice will oblige you to fight many hard battles; but it will be your best preparation not only for a soldier's life, but for that blessed time when peace shall once more prevail, and but one banner, even the star-spangled one, shall wave over the whole length and breadth of our land!

My story commences in the early autumn of 1860, before Abraham Lincoln's election to the Presidency was a fixed fact, and while the political world was seething and boiling, and passing through throes and convulsions, and unnatural comminglings, which remind one of the witch's caldron in Macbeth. And who can fail to see in Hecate's answer to the foul spirits she commanded, the counterpart of the commendation given by the leading men of that period to their tools and servants, —

"O, well done! I commend your pains,
And every one shall share i' the gains."

ECHOES FROM THE GUN OF 1861.

CHAPTER I.

THREE BROTHERS.

"But you will study, Thornton?"

"Study? Yes, when I'm in the mood for it, if that ever happens; but let's come to an understanding, Johnny dear. If I am a lazy dog, as all agree, I'm no hypocrite; and I'll tell you, my father-confessor, and brother St. John, just what I mean to do; that is, so far as such a floating straw as I am can be said to have any purpose in life. I'm going out to 'Old Kentuck,' to have a good time generally. Now don't look as if I was about to commit all the crimes in the decalogue. I scorn low vices, as you well know,— and, thanks to good influence at home, I'm inclined to good rather than evil; but here I am, a good-looking fellow of eighteen, with an average education, for my years, plenty of money in my own right, — thanks to Uncle Thornton Lester, — I'm not boasting, only telling facts, you know, with lots of time to settle down to the work of life you are always talking about, and doing, too. So I'm just going to have a right good time on Oscar's plantation this winter; take an observation of life and society in the Southwest, and then, — why, then, I'll promise to look about in earnest, and settle down to a work-a-day life. Will this suit you, Johnny boy? I hope so, for really I'm exhausted defining my position."

"I suppose it must, Thorny, only it seems a dangerous experiment for one of your temperament. You don't love to study nor to work; will you like either any better after six months or more of idle care?"

"Can't say, Johnny; but I'm bound to try the experiment. Now don't look so grave because I can't see life out of your conscientious blue eyes. I shall be a 'right smart chance of a man' yet; there's the 'makin's' of one in me, — I feel that intuition sure, — not that I care much about being anybody but just good, easy-going Thornton Lester Grey, with plenty of money and plenty of friends, and a mother and brother, either of whom are good enough to cover up my sins, and carry me straight through purgatory to paradise, but just for this reason, Johnny: no fellow with any heart at all could resist forever the example and persuasions of two such persons as mother and yourself. So, now, let a fellow alone, and be sure and be a good boy yourself this winter that is coming; and just practise the reverse of all the good advice you gave me, — *don't* study too hard, *do* lounge upon the sofa, &c. &c. You're a good old chap, after all, and rightly named St. John. Anybody else would be puffed up with conceit between two brothers such as you have, — a ne'er-do-well, like myself, and the incarnation of mischief and deviltry, like Horace. There's the scamp now."

And there he was, sure enough; for the door of the library where the brothers were sitting opened with a jerk, and closed with a bang, and with a loud, "Hollo, old Sleepy Hollow! here's the candy woman, — give me the two shillings you promised!" Master Horace stood, poised on one leg, beside Thornton's lounge. After receiving the promised money, he raised his voice to the highest pitch in that fashionable chorus —

"Bully for you! O, bully, bully for you! You're a regular trump, Thorn. Bully for — Oi, O, O!"

This sudden interpolation was called forth by a rap from Thornton; and the prolonged yell of mingled fun and vexation which followed, brought another actor on the stage, in the person of Mr. Grey. The door which opened to admit him also permitted the escape of Horace. It was made after his own fashion. Stooping down, he turned a somerset into the hall, and progressed in the same manner through it and down a dark passage into the back premises of the house, jostling against his

Aunt Esther on his way, putting one hand upon and almost crushing Margaret's pet kitten, and causing her to mew out most piteously, and finally knocking over a small girl waiting in the hall. Arrived at the kitchen, he startled the candy woman with a loud —

"Here's the ready! give us your saccharine compound, Mother Sweety; and good weight, too!"

After this little interlude, the brothers were silent for some time. Thornton reclined lazily upon a lounge, pulling the tassels of a sofa pillow; while St. John sat at a table, his head resting upon his hand, and an anxious expression upon his face. He looked the elder of the two, and far more mature; but this was doubtless owing in a great measure to the habits of his life. An injury received in early childhood had resulted in a permanent lameness, and threw him much upon mental resources. His sad look caught Thornton's eye, and he said —

"What a shame, Johnny, you should be lame, and I sound in limb, when you would so revel in freedom of body, and I would quite as lief spend two thirds of my time lounging as not."

"I don't agree with you, Thorny," said St. John, smiling. "You certainly never would have been good for anything if you had had the excuse of lameness for your laziness, while I should probably have out-Horaced Horace had I been free to go and come as I liked. I declare to you, Thornton, I have an intense sympathy with that boy's life and spirits, and always pity him when he gets into disgrace, and I feel as if I was a hypocrite to be thought so good and correct, when it's only circumstances that have made me better behaved than he is."

"Well, *that's* being conscientious with a witness! Circumstances may have made you inactive in body, but none that I can imagine would ever have taken the saint out of your heart, and put — well, mischief into it, or slang phrases into your mouth. By the way, that same Master Circumstance who has done so much for you, may take me in hand yet. Who knows but Oscar may be right, and that Southern talk is not all braggadocio, and that we may yet see fighting in our land of peace and plenty if 'Old Abe' is elected President? *That* would be circumstances with a vengeance, and would make or mar a nation. Imagine me a soldier boy, Johnny!"

And with these words, he rose and stood erect, his fine face lighted up with momentary enthusiasm, and his bearing that of one every inch a man. Momentary it was, however, for he did not believe there was any danger of a coming conflict; for, although there were the gathering clouds and the distant mutterings which foreshadowed the future tempest, few read the signs of the times aright; and Thornton Grey's conjecture was but a passing thought.

Mr. Grey, father of the three brothers whom I have so unceremoniously introduced to my readers, was a rich merchant in New York, residing during most of the year in a pleasant, attractive home on the Hudson River, some miles from the city. He had not retired from business, simply because his active habits precluded the possibility of his doing so while he had health and strength.

Mrs. Grey was a woman of refinement and culture, and a true, self-sacrificing wife and mother. The other members of the family, beside the brothers, Thornton, St. John, and Horace, were Esther St. John, Mrs. Grey's sister, and Margaret Duncan, an orphan ward of Mr. Grey's, a young girl of fifteen. Oscar, the eldest son, had married the heiress of a large plantation situated on the Ohio River, in Kentucky.

You hear a great deal about representative men, and such are held up to you as warnings, or examples, as the case may be. I am proud to believe Mr. Grey's to be a representative family, — representative of the grand ideas, and grander lives, that the fire of purification which our country is passing through has evoked into being. It is their glorious privilege to appear upon the broad stage of life in one of the grandest and most eventful periods of any nation's history. May it be mine to give a faint idea of noble qualities of character, aroused to action by the great alarum which sounded through the land, from one extreme to the other, in April, 1861.

CHAPTER II.

CIRCUMSTANCES.

The brothers were again interrupted by Horace's entrance, but this time he came shrinking in, cap in hand, with an odd expression upon his face, and strange to relate did not speak a word till St. John said, " What's the matter, Horace?"

" Matter enough; here's a pretty go. It isn't bad enough that Tom Bower's mother must be sick, and all the family have to be packed off to Europe, but Mr. Vernon must needs come and take the place. He's got a boy just about my age, deformed so that he can't walk at all, and what do you think? I was tearing through the park just now, with Cæsar after me, and between us we upset him in his little hand-carriage, and his head got cut quite badly. I helped the man who was drawing him get him to the house, and there I saw Mr. Vernon, and he said he and my father were good friends, and he hoped we boys should be too. Bother the luck, I say."

" Can't say that I quite see the relation between cause and effect this time, scapegrace," said Thornton. "I don't suppose you are obliged to be friends with this youngster unless you choose to be."

"You might see it if you'd ever take the trouble to think, Thornton," replied the boy, indignantly. St. John knows just what I mean. Do you think I'm such a mean chap as to knock over a poor lame boy that can't use his legs at all, and almost break open his scull, and then never go near him, or try to do anything for him? Guess you wouldn't if you'd seen his yellow curls and white face all sprinkled with blood, — ugh, it makes me sick to think of it."

Thornton was touched at the boy's evident feeling; but he didn't choose to let him see it just then; so he answered, "a lucky circumstance for you, Hor. A wild, rough boy, your senior and evil adviser steps off the stage, and presto, — on glides your good genius, in the shape of a gentle sickly child. O I see it all, — you reform in your manners, always take off your cap when you come into the room where ladies are, bow to and shake hands with mother's visitors, let Margaret and her kitten be at peace, hold aunt Esther's cotton and yarn for her; in short, become a pattern boy after the manner of Mrs. Nonesuch's. ('My boys never do so and so.')

"Then the invalid gains from you some of your superfluous spirits, and so, all through circumstances, we get a pattern boy, and Mr. Vernon a happier son."

"You may laugh as much as you like, Thornton,"

said Horace, quickly, " but don't hold up to me those Nonesuch boys. I wish their mother could see them kick, and pinch, and spit in the servants' faces, and know the mean tricks they're up to, out of her sight; such as lying, reading lessons off books, stealing candy and pencils. But St. John, whatever *am* I to do about this business?"

" Thornton is right, Horace. I dare say it will be a lucky circumstance for you. It will draw out the feelings of your kind heart; you can do so many things for the boy. You, such a stout, strong fellow, and he so weak and young. I'll go with you to-morrow to see him, and after that I dare say you'll not mind going by yourself. As for Tom Bowers," he added, with a quizzical look, " I wish him a pleasant voyage."

" You *are* the best kind of a fellow, St. John, to help a chap like me out of this scrape; guess I can behave under your wing, though I don't much fancy this sort of thing; goody boys ain't much in my line. I'll go and look over some games to carry to him. No, I'll run down to Hyde's first, to do that errand for mother, I forgot this morning. Here Cæs,— where are you, old Conqueror? Guess we've crossed the Rubicon to-day, and are in for it good or bad, fun or no fun."

And off he ran followed by Cæsar, boy and dog vieing with each other as to which should be the noisiest.

"If you have, as you say, Thornton, the 'makin's' of a man in you, I'm sure Horace has, too."

"Yes, yes, he has more heart than I thought. How pale he looked when he spoke of the blood! I answered him as I did because I was afraid he'd break down, and he's just the boy to think it a great weakness if he did."

Thornton spent the winter, as he proposed, with his brother Oscar. The effect of that winter upon his character will appear incidentally in the progress of my story. An extract from the commencement of his journal, kept while there, because he promised St. John he would do so, and one at the close, will give some idea of the change in his feelings, caused by circumstances.

October, 1860. "I am delighted with everything in this beautiful region; with this grand rolling country, its lofty woods and broad flowing river without, and the hearty hospitality within; with my brother's pretty wife and her charming southern manners. I must own this is a life after my own heart. Late to bed and later to rise; social visiting; none of your formal parties, but an unceremonious dropping in to spend day or night, plenty of servants, respectful and well trained, hunting, riding, and driving, on fine days; smoking, chatting, lounging or reading, on dull ones. No study yet. N. B. Not in the mood for it. O Johnny, Johnny, what will you say? And yet if 'the proper **study of mankind, is man,'** I 'm not altogether idle."

April, 1861. "I can scarcely believe my own eyes. When I went down stairs this morning, I saw over the glass in the sitting-room, a large cockade of red, white, and red; **and this after** yesterday's **news from** Fort Sumter! **Home,** home to-night, **where I shall find loyal hearts, and, God willing, my work too."**

"Speed Malise, speed ——"
* * * *
"The muster-place be Laurie Mead.
  Instant the time. Speed Malise, speed."

CHAPTER III.

THORNTON AROUSED AT LAST.

I MUST again bring my young friends into Mr. Grey's library where the whole family are gathered, including Thornton, who has just returned from Kentucky. He is giving an account of his journey home, and we will listen with the family circle and hear what he has to relate.

"Yes, father, I left Mulberry Grove, the 14th, for Louisville, intending to start for home that very night. But owing I suppose to the state of suppressed excitement I had been in for weeks, when I arrived at our good friend's Mr. Woodford's I was really sick. He sent me to bed at once, and for some days I was forced to stay there. Just imagine me chained to a sick-bed, my mind in a perfect chaos of feeling, and a furor of excitement raging in the city. My friends could not keep the state of things from me, for no one felt any security, in going to bed at night, that there might not be some violent outbreak before morning, for though as true and loyal hearts beat in Louisville as elsewhere in the Union, the strength of the opposing element was not known. Or rather it was known that there were in the city at that time many determined, reckless spirits, among them I believe some of that most chivalric band, Knights of the Golden Circle, and who only needed a resolute leader to do a vast amount of mischief. Our friend too might be a marked man, not only for his known loyalty to the Government, but for his interest in every cause of humanity. In case of difficulty I should only be a hindrance, so I made up my mind to start for home as soon as I could safely do so. As readily and kindly as I had been received and cared for, I was helped to get off, for both Mr. and Mrs. Woodford knew how impatient I was.

"But," said Mr. Grey, "you have not told us how you left Oscar and his wife affected at this change of affairs. Lina, I suppose, with her Southern education, prejudices, and interests might incline to excuse the South; but Oscar, I cannot imagine him, a Northerner, and *my* son, to have any sympathy with the South, or to take but one view of the matter."

"He has but one view of it, father," replied Thornton, bitterly; "what that view is will appear when I tell you that, the morning I left, a red, white, and red cockade was put up over the glass in the family sitting-room, and that Lina appeared at the breakfast-table with a breast-knot of the same colors. Our parting was none too brotherly, for I had swallowed my anger and indignation so often, had forborne and kept silence till forbearance and silence seemed no longer a virtue, that in reply to Oscar's dignified advice that I should not degrade myself by herding with Yankee pedlers and Northern abolitionists to sustain a rail-splitting President, I gave him not a piece, but the whole of my mind upon the subject. I scorned, however, to notice his fling at our President, farther than to say that the world would pronounce judgment upon him, and that it was not for Northerner or Southerner to say this or that. The verdict was to pass to a broader tribunal than ours; that I hoped I should be found worthy to fight side by side with the rank and file of my countrymen, in the cause of my country. *That* was my cause and the cause of every loyal heart in the land."

At this moment, while Thornton paused for breath, Horace, who had been listening with evident interest, but at the same time with an amused look of astonishment, cried out, "Bully for you, Thorn; three cheers and a tiger for the chap that speaks his mind." Then going towards him and looking at him from head to foot, he added, "I say, *is* this old Sleepy Hollow?

   'If this be I, as sure it cannot be,
    My little dog Tray'll know me.'

"Here, Cæs, old boy, come and see if this is Thorn. Yes, all right, go ahead."

All laughed at this most unexpected interruption, and Mrs. Grey said it was the step from the sublime to the ridiculous; and Thornton good-naturedly answered, "I don't wonder you're surprised, Horace. I'm astonished at myself. It's the latent St. John element coming out at last, in part I suppose but not entirely. There's a spirit abroad in the land one must be a heartless, witless fellow to withstand. Why, my journey home has been a grand triumphal procession. The only trouble was, steam was too slow for us. We should have travelled on the telegraph wires, only they wouldn't accommodate us; but I must tell you of the journey. Such a perfect spring morning as it was when I left Louisville to cross to Jeffersonville to take the cars to Cincinnati! It was one of those mornings when Nature was so lovely and peaceful, with all her fair promise of future growth and beauty, that it was hard to realize how disturbed men's minds were; yet you read it in every face. While we were crossing on a slow ferry-boat which sidled over la Belle Riviere at the rate apparently of one step back to two forward, it was amusing to watch the impatient looks of some of the passengers. One tall, rough-looking backwoodsman halloed to a passing craft, "I say, shipmate, couldn't you give this ere craft a shove across the river. I'm going home to list, but reckon old Abe'll 'bout have the fight settled up 'fore I git thar."

However, we did get across at last, and, once

started in the cars, the pace of the iron-horse was a little more suited to our feelings, though, as I said, all too slow.

I had seen flags waving in Louisville, and the grand national colors appearing in shop windows, in knots and bows for ladies dresses and children's uniforms, but I hardly looked to see such a display of flags of all sizes and material as greeted our eyes as we steamed along in sight at times of the Ohio River. For vessel, boat, or steamboat to be without the flag was the exception, and the nearer we drew towards Cincinnati the thicker we saw them, from steeple and belfrey, mansion-house or hut; now floating broad and full to the breeze, and again so simple and unpretending you could hardly see the red, white, and blue.

As I saw these beautiful colors over and over again, till everything seemed almost as if seen through a red, white, and blue medium, their significance flashed through my mind. Red, the very hue of the lifeblood so many would erelong give up to their country; white, the emblem of purity, — hence of truth and right; blue, heaven's own color.

Well, the end of all this excited state of feeling, for I'm not used to thinking and talking as St. John is, you know, it don't come naturally, but by inoculation, the end of it was a raging headache, which sent me to bed when I got to Cincinnati.

I was vexed enough at the time at the detention,

but glad when morning came and I got up bright and well, and still more glad when I found that part of an Ohio regiment were to be our companions for some distance. Just now no one travels except from business or necessity, and there were not many passengers in our car, so the soldiers filed in one after the other, in their new uniforms, bright equipments, with an expression on their earnest, manly faces that did me good to see. Some had wreaths upon their arms, others a knot of the loyal colors in a button-hole, and others still carefully held bouquets, all of which I suppose were parting tokens from wife, sister, or one dearer than sister. I sat for a while on the seat with their superior officer, a man about fifty years of age, and, as I should judge, an educated and professional man. He said Ohio had responded bravely to the President's call; she had given of her best, and that thousands more were ready and willing to go if needed. This regiment, he said, were of a superior class of young men; that they were from eighteen to twenty-five years of age, some few older, some of them married, and that all had left study or profitable business to enlist.

I had been so intent before we started in looking at the soldiers, that I noticed nothing else, and was quite startled when we were fairly on the way, at the demonstration which greeted us, and which followed us for two or three miles out of the city. Women waved their handkerchiefs from every door, window, and yard. Men and boys took off their hats and with hurrahs and shouts expressed their last good wishes, and children of both sexes waved miniature flags. It was as if we were a conquering army, so great seemed the jubilee!"

"Yes," said Mrs. Grey; "you saw the signs of jubilee; you did not see the sad and tearful faces you left behind."

"No, mother, and I don't think the boys thought much of it, either. One idea had the mastery, one idea beamed from their frank, determined faces, and found utterance from their lips, — devotion to the death to their country's service. By and by, in the toilsome march and the tedious camp life, they will think of those they left grieving at home. I was sorry enough when we parted with them. I dare say my account seems very tame, but it was grand to see, as you might suppose," he added, laughingly, to St. John, "since it has broken the spell which bound the enchanted knight. Now I am fairly entitled to a lounge on my old couch. Don't I look natural, now Thornton's himself again?. If you please, good friends, I'll listen to *you* now."

CHAPTER IV.

WISHES AND PLANS.

For a few moments no one spoke. St. John's flashing eye and flushed cheek told how heartily he entered into his brother's enthusiasm. Mrs. Grey looked fondly and sadly upon her son, knowing full well the sacrifice that was about to be demanded of her. Mr. Grey walked back and forth in the library, his countenance grave almost to sternness. Margaret wiped away the silent tears that she could not keep back, and Horace sat tilting his chair most precariously, evidently thinking very deeply for him. Miss St. John, who had been knitting while Thornton was talking, continued her occupation. She had not spoken at all, but her face had undergone curious transformations of alternate contempt, pride, indignation, and triumph as her nephew proceeded. She now broke the silence by laying her work in her lap and exclaiming, emphatically, "I wish I was a man."

Now the expression of this wish was so common with Aunt Esther that usually no one noticed it, unless it might be Horace, in some saucy aside to

Margaret, such as he wished so too, and then she would n't be spying upon him all the time. But she spoke now with so much feeling that Mr. Grey said, "Take heart, Esther; your work is coming. If I do not mistake, women will have a work to do in this war as grand as any, and that soon."

"Yes, yes, I know, — to stay at home to endure, to be tortured with anxiety, to weep while their nearest and dearest are suffering and dying. That's not my work; I'm neither patient nor good enough for it."

"There will be other work for you, Esther, — work that will try the stoutest heart and nerve of man or woman. The hospital which follows surely in the wake of war, will give you horrors enough. For the rest," he added, smiling, "you have the misfortune to be a woman, and I see no remedy for it."

"The hospital will do I suppose for want of anything better and more stirring, only how can I wait? I should like a chance at the enemy as some of the Revolutionary women had. I should like to fight these unnatural monsters who got up this Rebellion. I wish I had been in Baltimore when the villains fired upon the brave Massachusetts Sixth. But as to sitting here at home coddling myself, and knitting or even sewing for the soldiers, I can't do it when our liberties and our Government are in danger. I never have been over-fond of "woman's rights" women, but it seems hard to me, now, that when I should like to fight, and could fight too with any man of them all, I must stay at home and be nothing but a cross-grained old maid, grinding my own heart out; for truer words never spake poet than these : —

"A millstone and the human heart are driven ever round;
If they have nothing else to grind, they must themselves be ground."

"Well, auntie," said Thornton, "as father says, you'll soon have better work than that to do; and as for being cross-grained, why you'll nurse me most tenderly yet in the hospital; and for the matter of that, the Rebels too, if they need your nursing."

"The Rebels, never. Never; if I know my own heart there's not a particle of kindness or charity for them in it; yourself, yes, if you need it."

"You are going to the war, then?" said Mr. Grey to Thornton. "A superfluous question, however."

"I should think so, sir. I stopped at a recruiting office on my way through the city, and enlisted for myself or a substitute; the latter was a form till I could get the consent from you I was sure of."

"So soon," was all Mrs. Grey could say.

"Yes, mother; I knew you could not hold me back."

"And father, please let me go as drummer-boy," said Horace, emboldened to make the request he had been pondering during his tilts back and forth upon his chair, by the ready acquiescence of his parents in

Thornton's plans. Rub a dub, rub a dub, dub, dub; that'll be jolly. Say, father, may n't I go."

"I should think not; certainly not, till you have drummed a little more steadiness into yourself. It would be rather unfortunate if you should throw down your drum and run into the woods after squirrels, or to recreate yourself with standing on your head or turning somersets."

"By the way, Hor," said Thornton, observing the black expression of Horace's face; "What's become of little Verner? What's his name, Herbert? Did he prove a goody boy, as you feared he would?"

"He goody? why he's a trump; a face card; high, low, jack, and the game, altogether; as spunky, as peppery as Bob Sims, as merry as merry can be, and as good as — St. John."

"What rare combination of qualities. Pray, how do pepper versus pepper agree?"

"O, when he's mad I'm good as mother's pie, and still as mice when the cat's about; but then he never does get mad unless somebody's done something mean or dirty, and I don't go in for that you know. When I get mad at nothing he never says a word, only looks sorry, and I can't stand that look on his pale face. He says he'd go drummer-boy if he was sound in limb, that is, if his father'd let him. He's got all sorts of red, white, and blue things about, flags and rosets on things, and cockades; and my, how his eyes shine, and how red his cheeks are when he gets talking. He says, I play about and am so active that I do not know what it is to feel as he does, because I can't have so much time to think, and hear what older people say. When he's so excited I tell him he's a flag of the union himself."

"How's that?"

"Why, his eyes are blue, blue as the sky, and his skin is white, all but those red spots in his cheeks. Is n't there red white and blue for *you*? O, he's a bully chap, and I pity him so."

"Pity him, is n't he happy?"

"Why, yes, in a way. St. John'll tell you all about that. But do you think you'd be as happy as you would be if you wanted to be up and doing, and scrabbling about everywhere, and wrestling, and playing, and fighting (good-natured fighting) with other boys, and into all sorts of scrapes and fun, and then if you had n't any limbs to do all this with, and had just to keep quiet and be good, whether you wanted to or not. I say, do you think *you'd* like it?"

"No indeed, Horace, I should not. You pity him then because his free active spirit is chained down by his feeble body."

"Yes, that's it exactly. Now if he was a quiet, tame, good boy, I'd like him well enough I suppose, but I should n't care for him as I do now, and I should n't pity him. I hate to be pitied, and I never let on to him that I feel so. But I've heard and talked enough for one day, so here goes. Make a bow to Captain Grey, Cæs, and let's be off. I'm almost stifled."

"Stop humbug, *private* Grey at your service," said Thornton.

"Tell that to your granny," cried Horace, in a most incredulous tone as he closed the door, and tore through the hall, boy fashion.

"Never mind his manners, mother," said Thornton, as he observed the pained expression upon Mrs. Grey's face as Horace left the room. His heart is in the right place, and he's a noble little fellow in spite of slang. He has too much spirit to be decorous. The circumstance of that acquaintance has done something for him," he added turning to St. John.

"Thornton," said his mother, gravely, "what will circumstances do for you? I dread the peril your body will be exposed to when you go to the war, but I dread far more the peril to your soul when you are in daily intercourse with the profane and vicious."

"Not so much danger there as you think," interrupted Mr. Grey. "Men who go to a war like this, from the highest motives of patriotism and duty, have all their best qualities called forth. Their lower propensities are kept in check or it may be cured."

"Yes, mother; and beside that, the same circumstances that hinder one man in the right, help another. Now, by education and tastes, I am opposed to vice in any form, and I hope to turn these same circumstances to a good purpose."

"I'll tell you what," he added, rising and walking about. "I mean to keep a special journal for Horace, in which, beside putting down things that will amuse and interest him, I will particularly note instances where individuals have controlled circumstances, and brought good out of evil. Perhaps I'll sometimes give him the reverse side to make the right stand out more boldly. Poor fellow, he really thought you'd let him go as as drummer-boy, father, I do believe."

"The last thing I should consent to for a boy like him. He has a great deal to learn yet, before he can leave home in any capacity."

An hour later, as Thornton was still lying upon the lounge resting from his fatigue, and thinking over the change in his life that was so soon to take place, he heard Horace whistling to Cæsar in the hall. Presently he came to the door of the library and looked in. When he saw that Thornton was alone his careless manner changed at once, and coming up to his brother, said, "I say, Thorny, can't you persuade father to let me go as drummer-boy; I'm in earnest, I should like it of all things."

"No, Horace, I cannot, for two reasons;—one is, it would be useless to try, as his mind is fully made up on the subject; and then again it would be the worst place in the world for you."

"I can't see why. I'm tall and stout and strong for my age, fourteen, and I can bear as much fatigue as a man. I'm tired of this lazy life up here."

"You cannot bear as much fatigue as a man, and you are so restless and changeable, how could you conform to the strict rules of the camp and the field? Then, too, you know you are a fiery, hot-tempered chap; you'd be getting into difficulty all the time; and although I do not believe you are really low in your tastes, you do talk slang, and sometimes keep company that's not the best for you, and you don't know the temptations you'd be exposed to in the army. No, no, Horace, you ought not to think of going from home till you've got a little more of the good home can give you, if you'll take it. Father told you you must drum a little more steadiness into you before you thought of the army; and I tell you, you must fight many a battle with yourself, before you can do any other fighting, or even drum to incite others."

"Its mighty easy for you to talk, Thorn. A Sleepy Hollow like you never had any battles to fight. I wish you could be in my skin for a while and see how hard it is to be proper, and talk book, and keep still, and all that sort of thing. The very thing I want to go for is to use up some of my superfluous steam. I shall burst my boiler one of these days up here in this old stupid Dutchified place."

"No battles to fight," said Thornton, rising to his feet, — "why all the demons that torment you to your harm, of unrest, mischief, temper, and what not, are nothing to my one great enemy, call him what name you will, laziness, selfish ease, inertia, or

Sleepy Hollowism. Your foes that you must fight can be made your servants and aids if you subdue them, and will help you along in any cause in life. My foe has always to be contended against; he bids me lie still when I should be up and doing; idle when I should study; lounge, when duty says, what thy hand findeth to do, do with thy might. He is insidious too, and plausible, and would fain make me think that he keeps me out of harm. No, no, Hor, give me your enemies and you shall have my old man of the sea. Once saddled with such an incubus you'll soon beg for your little lively imps back again, and be quite content that all you have to do is to train them a little and make them help you."

"I never thought of that before; I always supposed my faults were the worst a fellow could have and the hardest to fight with, I hear so much about them; but now I see it must be a deal harder to want to do nothing all the time, and feel that you must and ought to be at work. Guess you may keep your old man of the sea; I always did pity poor Sinbad."

"I thought so," said Thornton. "Now you'll stay at home and fight more willingly wont you? We'll report to each other what progress we make; not perhaps in detail; but we'll let each other know about how we get along, I in the army, you at home in school, and we can draw our own inferences."

"Yes, I should like that; only don't you go to preaching to me. I get enough of that, one way and another. It'll be a blessed thing for me if Aunt Esther does go off to a hospital. I quite agree with her that there's no scope for her here."

"You'll miss her enough, if she does go, you ungrateful scapegrace," replied Thornton, with a laugh; "she's only too good to you."

"Yes, sir," was the reply, with a prolonged sound of the r that did n't quite amount to the slang expression in vogue; "that's just what I say, — too much of a good thing she gives me."

"Incorrigible!" said Thornton; "never fear that I shall waste preaching, as you call it, upon you; besides," he added, seriously, "there is no need. The record of my life in the army will be sufficient. If good, you will know it, and profit by it, I believe. I hope it may not be such as to injure you."

CHAPTER V.

DRILLING AND WAITING.

A FORTNIGHT later found Thornton in camp, near Washington, really entered upon his soldier's life. He had adhered to his resolution of enlisting as a private, although his father could easily have procured a commission for him. But he said he knew nothing of the duties of an officer, that he was not fit to command, and that he would go into the ranks and earn promotion before he accepted it. His father readily assented to his wishes in this respect, feeling that his judgment was correct; and his mother, though she sighed over his anticipated privations, as loving mothers will, said no word to dissuade him from his purpose. Fondly and tenderly she looked after her brave boy, whom she hardly knew to be hers, in the altered character in which he now appeared; and with her prayers and blessings he had gone forth from the home of his childhood, as thousands have gone beside him, — some to be almost miraculously preserved from peril; some to hunger and die in Southern prisons; some to win glory and honor on the field; some to be taken in strange and mysterious ways while yet their young brows were wreathed with unfading laurels of noble deeds, **and** all to a certain life of exposure and hardship. Such portions of his journal as were written expressly for Horace I shall lay before my young readers.

May, '61. Well, Hor, the Rebs did n't take Washington; did n't march on to Philadelphia and New York, to the tune of

"See, the conquering hero comes!"

did n't have a good time generally pillaging these cities; did n't dictate a peace upon their own terms, and then settle down as the aristocratic race par eminence, and found a mighty empire, of which slavery was the chief corner-stone, before whose might and power Yankee tinkers and Northern mudsills and abolitionists should bow in reverence, thankful for being allowed the privilege of submission.

I say they did n't do all this. Why?

Simply because, literally and metaphorically, the United States Government was too many for them, — because the American heart beats true and loyal to the good old flag, and thousands upon thousands are ready to fight and if need be to die under its folds.

How astounded the Southerners are at this great uprising of the North! I must laugh when I think how they have reckoned without their host. I used to hear them talk, last winter, in their arrogant fashion, and say that, in case of a collision with the North, there would be a large party there who would join them, — that, as the Yankees were not a nation of gentlemen, accustomed to field sports, and to avenging insulted honor, they were no fighters, and that one Southerner was equal to five Northerners, — that while they should send their best blood into the field, the flower of Southern chivalry, we at the North should depend upon foreign mercenaries and low mudsills to do our fighting.

All this stuff the majority of the people South have been taught to believe!

Now put on your magical glasses, and come and look with me at our encampment, and judge for yourself whether we are in earnest or not. From this hill we look down upon the white tents which, scattered far and near, form the present lodging of the Army of the Potomac. Some of these tents are in thick clusters, in the open country; others gleam out through forest-trees. In open spaces you see men in squads, companies, and regiments, infantry and cavalry, going through all the various evolutions which constitute the drilling of a great army. Look at them! You can count them by hundreds and thousands, and know that you are looking upon men of all ranks and conditions in life, animated by one spirit and one purpose.

You're a bright boy, Horace, so comment is needless. We're bound to conquer. Some of our wise ones say it'll not be done in a hurry, — that we underrate the force and earnestness of the enemy; but we boys most of us think one good drubbing from our army'll bring them to terms.

Tell St. John I've had an opportunity already of seeing how some of our boys use circumstances. We have a good deal of leisure, and many of our officers, and some of the men who have influential friends, spend a great deal of their time in Washington, — evidently, for the most part, to their injury. Removed from the restraints of home, and exposed to the temptations ever springing up in their path, too many make a poor use of their privileges, and enter into dissipation that would shock their friends at home, if they knew of it. Inaction in camp is bad for all. Some of us, who have no inclination for dissipation, stay quietly on here; and others, who are strongly tempted, bravely resist. Such are fighting their hardest battles now. But I don't forget I'm not to preach, and that you want to know about my companions in arms. Opportunely for the introduction, Pat Finnegan cries out, —

"Be my sowl, it's meself that's tired of this ploy fightin'!"

"That's so, Pat," breaks in Jake Brown's rough voice. "I come to fight, and ef I don't git a chance soon to pull my trigger, I'd a tarnation heap rather be in the woods among the pine trees to hum."

"You'll have fighting enough soon, old boy; and maybe then you'll wish you had some of your old friends to protect you. A tree's a good screen," said John Trimmer, whom, for certain reasons, we call Brag.

"Maybe," said Jake, dryly; "but for lack of a tree I'll git behind you. I can stoop, and your back is broad enough to shield a chap."

"I'm afraid you'll hardly do that, for I shall be in the thickest of the fight."

"Thickest? dare say," growled Jake, "leaving out the s."

"Good for old Holdfast," roared another of our boys, Jim Whittier, who is a wag in his way, and whom I don't know as fighting will ever make sober.

Jake Brown is a Maine backwoodsman, who happened to be in New York at the time of the call for troops, and who enlisted at once, without waiting to return home, and whom we call Holdfast.

Ned Howe, of our set in the city, but now my superior officer, to whom I am obliged to be very respectful in public, is not going on very well. He's one of those fellows our present life will make or mar. Just now he goes to the city too often for his own good. He tries to keep away, but says he can't resist temptation.

Then there's Lee Waters, a pale, delicate boy,

who looks as if he ought to be at home, under his mother's care, — only, poor fellow, he hasn't any; instead of which, he shrinks from no hardship, and never complains, though he coughs night and day. He's almost insanely patriotic. We'd pet him if we dared; but it would never do.

In strong contrast to Lee, is Joe Clarke, whom we call Dub, for short. He's an out-and-out feather-bed and sugar-candy boy; so Jim Whittier called him double-refined sugar, which we abbreviated as above. He's always groaning and moaning, and telling how he had things at home, and tormenting our lives out with his complaints. In return, he gets knocks and slaps, not a few, — I mean with the tongue. "Does your mother know you're out?" "Lullaby, sweet lullaby! hush, my darling, mother is near!" Condolences, offers of lozenges and dainties, and mock petitions to headquarters for a supply of Mrs. Winslow's Soothing Syrup, constitute our revenge upon him.

Our wit may not seem to you very brilliant, though some of us do get off good things occasionally. It wouldn't stand drawing-room criticism; but in camp, or on the march, with the accompaniments of droll looks and high spirits, it's not contemptible. As a rule, I should say, our boys, and I mean all with whom I come in contact, are resolved to be jolly, and get all the fun they can out of their hardships. Exceptions there are, of course, — fault finders, croakers, and effeminates, — but they are few, and the jollies are in the ascendant. And not a whit the less serious are they about the great business in hand, for this same jollity. It is, in fact, a legitimate result of their earnestness. Resolutely and cheerfully they have started to conquer, or die, and all petty annoyances are scorned or turned to fun.

Well, besides jokes and fun, we have games, and chats, and long yarns, and political discussions, and reading and writing, to fill up the odd hours when we're not drilling, or on duty, or polishing our equipments.

There's one thing about camp life: it does for a man what school does for the boy. Each one stands upon his own merit. Shams don't go down; and if conceit does n't get taken out of a fellow mighty quick, it is n't the fault of the boys.

"How do I like camp fare?"

First rate. To be sure, we get some luxuries now we shan't always have, when "we're marching along," and as we penetrate further into Virginia's sacred soil; but hard tack and salt pork and beef are not to be despised, with the appetites we bring to them.

"How do I like my bed?"

That't first rate, too, whether on the ground or the soft side of a board. It seemed a little hard at first, and made my bones ache; but that was all owing to mother's petting at home. Now it's quite soft and refreshing.

I'm summoned to drill, — a business I'm as tired of as Pat and Holdfast. Never mind, we are to have real fighting soon, and I shall write you a jubilant account of victory.

CHAPTER VI.

BATTLE AND DEFEAT.

JULY, 61. I was premature in my **boast, Horace.** We've had a battle; but you will hear **no** jubilant sounds **of** victory. No. Before this **the** wail of defeat has gone over the land, and perhaps you may have already blushed for the army of the Potomac, which went out with martial music, flying banners, and exultant hearts, in full faith of speedy victory, and which returned defeated, dispirited, **and** panic-stricken.

But you need not blush for us, though you **may** grieve for and with us. You must remember, that, though **ours** was a large and powerful army, it was an undisciplined one, the majority **of** us the three years' troops just enlisted, and that we met a comparatively practised foe.

Errors **of** judgment there doubtless **were, and** mistakes also. Perfectly organized armies **do not** grow up like Jonah's gourd **in** the night. But a braver, truer, more patriotic set of men never **went** out to do battle for a righteous cause **than** this *our* army of the Potomac. I say this in spite of the exaggerated reports of our defeat, or disgraceful rout, as some will have it.

But I must begin at the beginning, if I can go back to anything so tame, after our late terrible experience. When orders came for us to break camp, taking three days' rations in our haversacks, and leaving behind all superfluous baggage, they were received with wild acclamations.

Pat roared out, "And shure it's meself that's just aching for a foight; we'll show 'em how it's done in the ould counthry."

Old Holdfast grunted, "Good news at last," and showed his satisfaction by the gleam in his dark eye, and his prompt movements. Brag talked big, and swaggered about, but *looked* blue enough.

Lee's cheeks burned brighter than ever with the loyal color, and his eyes fairly danced in his head, and he moved restlessly about, hither and thither, and could not be persuaded to keep quiet and save his strength for time of need.

As for Jim Whittier, he leaped and danced about like a wild creature, performing all sorts of ridiculous antics and figures, little dreaming, poor fellow, how it would be with him on the battle-field.

As for myself, I must have had something of the old Sleepy Hollow look about me, for, while I was deliberately putting my equipments in order, Jim came up to me, and gaving me a huge poke between my ribs, said, "Look alive, man! do you belong to this generation or the past? what kind of a face is that to carry to battle? Meditation to the dogs; action's the word," and, as he spoke, he gave a leap forward with his bayonet fixed, as if charging the enemy, and almost ran it into Dub, who just then appeared. He did disarrange the cloak Dub had just then gracefully thrown over his shoulders, thereby causing the latter infinitely more disgust than the narrow escape from cold steel had induced **fear**. Should n't wonder, after all, if our double refined should prove to have plenty of pluck.

Jake says a few nights sleeping in the mud, and a few days' short rations, and one tough fight, will make a man of him.

But to the battle. If you are as eager to hear as we were to be in it, you'll not care **for small** details.

To our intense mortification, we were for some time in the rear, seeing the signs and hearing the sounds of a terrific contest raging, and doing our best for the poor wounded fellows brought to us. O, it was terrible to see them, with their ghastly and bloody faces, some convulsed with agony, others rigid in stern determination. Some raved and screamed in their extremity, others bore their sufferings with compressed lips and knitted brows. **One** poor lad, whose wound was mortal, cried out "Mother! mother!" in tones piteous to hear. Another, with a countenance distorted by pain, and fierce as that of a savage warrior, yelled out to us,

"Go to the front, you lazy devils, orders or no orders, — shoot, stab, kill, kill, kill, — that's what you're here for," and with the last word he sank back insensible, the blood gushing in torrents from his side.

"O, my country! my country!" cried another. "God help you! brother fighting against brother. O, my poor head; where am I, at home, or where? O," as a kind hand bound up the wound in his temple, "I remember now. Father in heaven, spare me for my country."

But there was one boy from a Massachusetts regiment whose agonies I shall never, never forget. He was horribly wounded; so disfigured, I don't believe even a mother's love could have recognised him. At first we thought he was raving, for he kept repeating, "Cain killed his brother, and God's curse was upon him; and I, I killed my brother, I saw him fall. O, brother, brother, what will our mother say?" These and words of similar import he repeated over and over again. At last, a young man, whose right arm had been shot off, and who belonged to the same company, found voice to say — "You couldn't help it, Ned; you didn't know;" and adding, to me, "Yes, he shot him down. I think he knew him before the ball took effect. Who knows how many brothers are to perish in the same cruel way? Ned is so tender-hearted, it will break his heart; brave as a lion too."

Poor Brag, I could n't but pity him from the bottom of my heart, though I was so vexed with him, too. I could willingly have pitched him down hill into a brook, and left him there to cool his fright. The sight of the wounded, their terrible disfigurement, and a stray ball which now and then found its way to us, terrified him almost out of his wits. At last, after a shot which came very near hitting him, he actually fainted away. Lee looked as if he could have killed him on the spot, and Holdfast said, " Poor chap, he 's enermost skeered to death; it 's wus than the bullets. He 'll do better though when we 're in the thick of it."

But our time was coming, and I was glad of it, for I felt sick almost, looking at the poor wounded fellows, and longed to be at work.

I am writing of that fearful Sunday, you know; that Sunday when you were at home quiet and peaceful, or listening to the word of God in his house of prayer, while we ——— .

Come with me to this rising ground, look around. It is just before we go into action; our nerves are braced, and our heart is steeled to anything.

Holdfast says " there 's hot work ahead. I come to fight, and I guess here 's a chance to do it pretty thoroughly. Ef I git hit it can't be helped, I calculated to run my risk of that, but I hope I'll do some tall fightin fust; thunder an lightnin but them rebs *is* in airnest."

Lee looked like an evil spirit; and he swore between his set teeth, if orders did n't come to move soon, he 'd go without.

I say nothing, but I look and I ask myself are these men or demons I see yonder; are they men with human hearts and human affections, or are they demons let loose from the infernal regions, and holding high revel on this fair spot of earth?

Far as the eye can reach are sights of blood and warfare; far as the ear can hear are sounds echoing, reverberating from distant points of action only fainter duplicates of those we hear around us.

There are men arrayed against men, brother against brother, shooting, stabbing, and the terrible artillery thundering over the smaller rain of shot and bullet, and doing deadly execution too, for legs and arms are severed from bodies and fly through the air in a manner horrible to behold. Yonder in the valley, from heavy clouds of smoke, come the lightning flashes of artillery and rifles. To the right is the fierce onset of opposing cavalry, the horses only one degree less human in their looks than their riders; and just beyond the equally fierce hand to hand combat of the infantry. On yonder hillside gleam out the rifle and bayonet. Like us, the men are waiting for orders to a certain point. And, O sight of horror, down in the valley are heaps and heaps of wounded and slain, horse and rider, friend and foe; and over all still sweeps on the deadly fight. The sounds, how shall I describe them? The whiz, whiz, of the bullets, the leaden rain, the thunderous roar, the almost human scream of the murderous shells, the heavy tramp of horses, the hoarse cries of leaders urging on their men to victory or death; the shrieks, groans, yells; the dreadful curses, the agonized petitions to God for mercy, and wild and fierce the martial music resounding through all this, are almost stunning to a looker-on. But I am a looker-on no longer, our orders have come at last; down the hill to the left, to aid a wornout regiment who have fought bravely for hours. Down we go; double, almost double-double quick, so eager are we; and now — we are on the spot, yonder our foe, a fresh regiment, fresh as ours and every whit as determined. No time to look about now; load, fire, and slay; load, fire, and slay, as fast as many as we can, — that's our work, and we do it, bravely too; never flinching, only drawing closer and closer as man after man of us is shot down and falls into the human heap at our feet. I am almost insane in my desire to load and shoot faster, still faster.

Those fearful sounds but now so terrific to my ears are but the fit accompaniment to my excited feelings. To all the wild din of war my heart beats back in throbs as wild. Still we fight, and still they fight; but for one moment they slacken, an alarm in the rear as we afterwards heard was the cause; that one moment gives us the advantage, we pursue it, and we pursue them, the small remnant that remains, till pursuit becomes too dangerous, and we look about for another foe, taking breath the while and trying to discover who are left of our brave boys. Lee Waters, whom I had seen fighting like a devil incarnate, is not wounded, but he stands pale and panting, his hands close pressed against his side.

Brag, I had seen him fighting as bravely as any, falls into his white fits again the moment immediate pressure is over. Holdfast looks coolly at his left arm, slightly wounded in the fleshy part of it, and says, "better luck than I thought for," and turns me round and examines the wound in my shoulder, a mere graze, looks at the bullet-mark through my coat on the left side, and says, "a near thing that."

Poor Jim is missing, and we find him presently in a heap of killed and wounded, and Brag gladly helps one of the other boys carry him to the rear. But we had barely time to get him off, for the battle surged towards us again, and we were once more drawn into the midst of it. Soon the cry went forth that the enemy was disheartened and had fallen back. So they were for the moment; and perhaps if the war had been man's war only, we should have gained the victory and settled down once more into supine ease, quite convinced of the insignificance of our foe. But the war is God's war, and He saw fit to humble us that we might be aroused to greater efforts. His eye had been upon us all day, really so it had seemed to me, as I caught a glimpse of the sun riding high in the heavens, the only object that was unaffected by the din and carnage raging below.

Feebly as I have described these horrors to you, you must have had enough of them; it was the same thing over and over, only as the day waned the contest grew hotter and hotter, so sure were we of victory, when suddenly came the appalling tidings that the enemy had been reinforced, and that our army was in full retreat. The next report was that a panic had seized our troops and that they were flying before the enemy. It was too true and too bad, and yet not so bad as has been told you, for the whole army was not panic-stricken, as was proved by their preventing the enemy, flushed with their unexpected victory, from following us. Our army bore the stigma of being panic-stricken, when crowds and crowds of people who were not of us, teamsters, spectators, idlers, helped to swell our numbers, and to add tenfold to the terror and confusion of the hour. I do not deny that many of our men were panic-stricken. All are not heroes, and some who fight the most bravely or even recklessly under the pressure of the excitement of the battle-field, are most easily intimidated when a cry of panic is raised. Remember too the terrible strain of hard fighting and anxiety that had been upon us so long. The nerves of the bravest might be supposed to give way a little, so long as men are men and not gods. As a resolute war-cry will sometimes rally a disheartened host, so too will a panic spread with lightning-like rapidity; for we men, proud as we are of our manliness, are sympathetic creatures after all. But I leave all explanations to those who, sitting at home in slippered ease in the drawing-room, or lounging on balconies at watering-places to catch the cooling breeze, tell men how this or that might have been avoided, and the battle won. Let me remind such of the old copy, " Circumstances alter cases," and suggest that a burning July sun, hard fighting as ever was done, nerves excited almost to madness by the horrible surroundings of a battle-field, are less favorable to cool clear judgment than their adjuncts.

Excuses too for our defeat I leave to those of our army who think we need to make them. Bravely and nobly fought our army of the Potomac on the field of Manassas, as thousands of crushed hearts and mourning homes bear solemn witness. Greater love hath no man than this, that a man lay down his life for his friends.

Our lives were freely given by us to our country. Those of us who were spared made the offering as freely as those that were taken. But this troublesome scratch on my shoulder worries me a little, so good night, Horace. If you have had a Bull Run or Manassas battle, I hope you came off victor.

CHAPTER VII.

AFTER THE BATTLE.

JULY, '61. The last pages in my journal were hastily written as soon after our inglorious flight from Manassas as I could catch a moment's leisure, and I now add a few incidents which occurred afterwards, that may interest and amuse you.

I shall not describe our retreat, for are not the accounts thereof to be found in the chronicles of the day? I should despair of giving you anything as stirring as the sensation descriptions you may find in any of the penny journals, or anything more reliable than the accounts of faithful reporters. There was a ludicrous side to it too, if we had been in the mood to look at it. As it was, the rapid and undignified skedaddling of some of our spectators, and the intense anxiety depicted upon their countenances, gave the assurance that they had seen the elephant, even beyond their desires. Some of them, I think, will never go out again to see the spectacle of a battle.

Of the boys I have named to you, Jim is the only one severely wounded, and the surgeon thinks he will recover, and be in fighting trim, when the cry comes, we so long to hear, — on to Richmond.

Brag hardly deserves his name now, and is plainly trying to retrieve his character. He has been put upon picket duty several times and has acquitted himself well, though with his nervous terrors I know it must be hard work for him. By the way, Horace, I hope you keep a picket guard well posted in your camp. If it is far better to be on the watch for a foe than to be taken unawares. I long to hear how your fight comes on. Remember, " greater is he that ruleth his own spirit than he that taketh a city."

But to return to our boys. Lee has had an attack of bleeding at the lungs. We all thought he would die, but he is slowly recovering. I see both him and Jim occasionally at the hospital, and Lee seems as vindictive as ever, nay more so; for he thinks our defeat a burning shame, and showers down abuse upon all in power and command without stint.

Holdfast goes on in his old steady way, only " more so." He's likely to become Holdfast in the superlative degree, for I never saw one more thoroughly in earnest. As he says of himself, " when I fust jined the army it was more cause I kinder thought I'd like a change than any great grudge I had agin' the rebs, an' I don know's I feel any bigger grudge now than afore; but thunder an' lightin', I'll fight's long's I hold out for the old flag. I never knowed I keered so much about it afore; but when I seed the enemy fightin' aginst it, I kinder choked all up, and felt's ef I rather die for it than live without it. An' now my mind's made up to fight's long's the war lasts, an' ef Sally to hum keers enough bout me to wait an' take the chances of arms shot off, ef I don't lose my head too, why she *can* wait. Ef she don't want to, she need n't.

I said, I thought Sally would wait and be proud of her hero.

"I don't mean nobody shall be ashamed on me, and Sally's a plaguey smart gal. She can take care of herself too while I 'm away, an' that 's somethin.' Guess nobody 'll come sparkin' round her ef she don't want em. Ef she does, why I 've my country left."

The deep sigh that accompanied this latter suggestion rather contradicted his assumed stoicism. I confess I never dreamed that Holdfast had a true love in the wilds of Maine. He don't look it.

As for Pat, he's a case to keep in bounds when we 're not hard at work some way. He thinks drilling a "pitiful mane business, and shure," he says, "I knows how to foight without so much bother about it; its jist natral to meself to have a shindy. An' what do yees think; I jist ached for a real foight yestreen, after the play foight we 'd had, and so I was compilled to give John McGee a knock in the side of his head, and what do ye think the big spalpeen did? Why he intered a complaint aginst me; an' when I tould the Captain it was to keep me hand in jist, I did it, he would n't take it for an apologee at all at all, an' so I was forced to spind the nicht in meeditation, I was."

"Meditation, Pat?" asked one of the boys; "How was that?"

"Och, an' shure, in a small shanty by mese'f, an' niver a bit of lave to go an' come as I liked!"

Dub has got the grumbles pretty well taken out of him, and has started off on a new tack, and boasts of his feats of war. We treat him like the coxcomb he is, and by and by he'll come out right.

You ask me if battle is like boys' fights, on a large scale. For myself, I can answer, not a bit of it. You beat Tom, or pitch into him, as the phrase is, because you have a special grudge against him, or because he has done some wrong you choose to right in that fashion. It's Tom you have a spite against; it's Tom you wish to pummel. We go into battle with no individual grudge or enmity. We fight not for ourselves, but for our country. We have no scores to settle with conscience, as you boys have, or ought to have. We are right, and we are fighting for the right. The fact, so dreadful in its naked reality, that we are shooting, stabbing, and killing so many men, is not at the time a reality to us. We are doing a needful work for our just cause. That is the pre-eminent thought, and the inspiring one. This is why fighting in the ranks is so much easier to a true-souled man than single hand-to-hand encounters, or deliberately shooting down a man when you are on guard, if your duty requires it. In the latter case, it is hard to get over the feeling that you are, in one sense, a murderer, though you know you are only doing your duty. The mystery of war, in this nineteenth century, with all our boasted progress in the arts and sciences, and our high civilization, I do not pretend to fathom. Still less can I reconcile it with the doctrine of Him who came to bring peace and good will on earth. I only know that to me this seems a righteous, God-appointed war; and, though dimly, as a vision far off, yet can I see in it results which shall affect the whole civilized world.

I have spoken of feelings which influence me, and which I know influence others, in combat; as, for instance, Holdfast, who fights as bravely as man can, and yet is tender as a woman to the wounded Rebels with whom he has anything to do.

But all do not feel as we do. Lee fights as if every man in the ranks was a personal foe, and I should pity the poor fellow who asked mercy of him. There are others like him, doubtless. I am sure he must have some private grudge, that has changed the milk of human kindness into gall. Some day I shall find out about it.

No, no, Horace; although war is a horrible evil, yet thousands upon thousands who are engaged in it are of earth's best and noblest. Do not make it an excuse for boys' fights. It won't hold good, even on the side we think wrong and aggressive. The majority of our enemies are self-deceived, or misled by their leaders, and have as firm belief in the righteousness of their cause as we have of ours.

I know no bright side, no redeeming feature, in boys' fights. I have never been able to enjoy the books you read with so much avidity, describing battles and "set-to's" between the boys in English schools. I believe there are other and far nobler ways of making the youth of a country brave and hardy. I do not blame the boys, however. I know of no slavery worse than the system of fagging, through which the boys of England must pass. I know no better school for turning out sneaks or bullies, or fighters according to the original character of the boy. Tell me, if you can, one noble feeling ever inspired by a boy's quarrel and fight, unless it be a fight to protect the weak from the oppression of the strong.

As for me, when I fight in battle,

"A thousand hearts are great within my bosom;"

so fight I, as they bid me, for God and my country.

When I commenced the account of the battle, while I was yet a looker-on, I asked myself, as you will remember, if they were men or demons upon whom I looked. Now I can answer, that all men do not look like demons when they are in battle. Ah, no! I have caught glimpses of "holy ardors," and noble enthusiasm, which have almost transfigured to something divine the human face out of which they shone. But enough of this. I hope I've not transgressed, and verged upon a "preach."

We take prisoners, of course; and I am going to

relate to you a somewhat laconic conversation which took place between a regular scion of the F. F. V.'s and myself. He was really a Southern aristocrat, educated and refined, but prejudiced withal, — such a young man as you have seen, in times past, at father's table, a courteous, polished guest.

He was standing leaning against a tree, looking rather fiercely around him, but every inch the gentleman.

I addressed a few remarks to him, in courteous tones, and offered to bind up his bleeding arm till the surgeon came. He refused, saying it was nothing; and then, eyeing me earnestly for a few moments, inquired, —

"Are there many in your army like yourself?"

"In what respect?"

"In your position in life."

"Thousands!"

"What do you fight us for?"

"For the love of country, and yonder stars and stripes."

"*We* fight for our homes and hearths, and to repel Northern invasion."

"Do you read the newspapers?"

Haughtily: "Of course."

"Who commenced the war, fired the first shot?"

"We were compelled to it. We had asserted our independence, and did n't want your troops in our ports, in and upon our territory."

"Who had troops, arms, and ammunition ready for this struggle?"

"We, to be prepared for this very invasion."

"Whew! Yet you, — your press, rather, — say that we are a nation of cowards, mudsills, worshippers of the dollar, Yankee pedlers, &c. Such a foe would hardly require such extensive preparation."

"We expected to intimidate you, and save bloodshed."

"What do you think *now?*"

"We have beaten you."

"Yes, *to-day*. But that is evading the question."

"Well, we think you *can* fight."

"Yes, we *can*, and we *shall*."

"We are prepared for Lincoln's hordes."

"Excuse me, but I must laugh."

Defiantly: "At what, sir?"

"At that expression. I used to read about Attila and his hordes; and to hear these words applied to our Northern troops, mustered by our good Father Abraham! Excuse me, but isn't it of the hifalutin' style of talk?"

"I admit that you are a better set of men than we expected to meet; but we suppose you have taken all your best men to meet this emergency."

"You shall see."

Defiantly again: "Many or few, good or bad, we are ready for you, and shall fight to the death!"

"Be sure; so shall we."

"But we fight for our homes and hearths; you for an idea."

"A grand idea, granting that to be the fact."

"Yes, it's plain *you* think it so. I saw you in the heat of the fight. Our company opposed yours; and when I saw how you and others fought, I thought better of you, as men of pluck, than I ever did before. But I detest your wicked invasion, and your meddlesome interference with us and our rights. Still, I must admit that there are *some* men of honor, and gentlemen, among you. But we have all our best blood in the field, probably far outnumbering yours, of equal rank."

I looked askance, at this, at a "poor white," who, also a prisoner, lounged upon the ground, — a wretched object, but the tenth part of a man in appearance, — at least, as I reckon manhood.

"Yes," he said, answering my look, "we have such men in our army; but we have, too, the flower of Southern chivalry."

He was a prisoner, and I thought it ignoble to taunt him, or I should have said, "It will take a great many flowers to counterbalance such weeds as that;" so I made him no reply, but went off to find the surgeon; for his increasing paleness proved that his wound was more severe than he was willing to acknowledge.

CHAPTER VIII.

HORACE POSTS HIS PICKETS.

MEANTIME, while Thornton is busy in camp, or on the field, what are the family at home about?

Up and doing, every one.

Mr. Grey gives freely of his time, his money, and his correct and mature judgment, to help on the cause of right.

So also does Mrs. Grey, in her sphere; and most bravely, too, she bears the burden of anxiety for her son's safety, — so bravely, those who never look beneath the surface call her a Spartan mother, and wonder at her cool and calm manner. No eye but that of the All-Merciful One sees her agony and grief. *He* sees, and pities and strengthens her; and she goes on with the work that her hand findeth for her to do, and in it she gains the best relief to her anxious heart.

Esther St. John has found her work, — not quietly at home, like her sister, but in hospital service; and so engrossed is she in it, that she has no time to regret that she is not a man, — for, in fact, in this service, if anywhere, a true woman has no time for idle lamentations.

Margaret knits socks and makes shirts for the soldiers, and fashions for them the prettiest little thread-cases, weaving in with her stitches many a kind wish for the soldier-boy, fresh and warm from her tender heart.

Horace is trying, too, to learn to knit; but I will tell you, confidentially, that I do not think he will succeed in helping the soldiers much in this way. He is too restless. He drops stitch after stitch, and as they go down, he looks despairingly at them, and begs Margaret to take them up scientifically. He can't be made to see through the intricacies of seam and narrow, and slip and bind, and finally tosses his knitting in the air, and rushes out of doors for a vent to his pent-up spirits, and races with Cæsar. It is true, I am getting before my story, for it is now July, and Horace did n't take his knitting-lessons till autumn; but I am telling you, in a general way, how they all worked, in one fashion and another.

As for St. John, he possessed his soul in patience as long as he could, and contented himself as best he might in helping his father and mother, in small ways; but when the second great uprising of the loyal North came, he could forbear no longer. So, one day, he sought Mr. Grey, and said, —

"Father."

"Well, my son, what is it?"

"I *must* do more for my country than I am now doing. You know Sam Drew, sir!"

"Yes, St. John; what of him?"

"He is clerk in the city, and gets a good salary, upon which his mother and young brothers and sisters depend mainly for their support. He would gladly go to the war. He's a stout, strong, healthy fellow. His mother will not refuse her consent. May I take his place, do his work for the benefit of his family, and let him go?"

"Have you thought this matter over in all its bearings, St. John?"

"Yes, sir, in all."

"Very well, then, I do not object, and will make but one condition: if your health fails, I must find another to do the work. The sacrifice you make to your taste, I know you will readily bear."

"A small one, sir, to one who longs to give his life to his country. You have removed the only obstacle by promising to fill my place if my health fails."

You see St. John made neither his youth nor his delicate health an excuse for doing nothing. He could not do what he longed to do with all the earnest ardor of an enthusiastic nature, — go forth, with Thornton, to active service; but here was a work he could do for the cause, — a most distasteful work, it is true, and one requiring him to give up his books and studies, — for all the leisure he would have he must now devote to rest and exercise, — yet he was ready to do it. Did not he control circumstances, and nobly, too?

Thornton's suggestion to Horace, that he should fight battles at home, while he was fighting abroad, pleased that restless lad's fancy. No other form of suggesting to him that he must learn to be his own master before he could hope to control others would have had so much influence with him.

"Pooh!" he said, "I'll let Thorn see I can fight myself, as well as another chap. I've had a few skirmishes before now with Horace Grey, that nobody, unless it's mother, knows anything about. I mean to have a regular pitched battle next time there's occasion."

There soon was an occasion; but he shall tell his own story to you as he told it to Thornton.

July, '61. Well, old chap, you *are* in a fair way to get all the Sleepy Hollow taken out of you. I'm following your course, and that of the other boys, pretty closely, and I guess I shall see what you all make out of circumstances. Mother told me your plan. I'm glad you let me find out for myself, and don't give me a little preach every now and then, saying, "You see how this and that caused t'other," as if a boy of common sense couldn't tell that two and two make four! Give my respects to Pat, and tell him I shake hands with him, and have longed many a time to pitch into somebody or other.

I s'pose 't is n't magnanimous (I *can* spell the word, and that's the rule, I believe, for using big ones) to triumph over a beaten man, so I won't do it; but, instead, I'll tell you about my Bull Run and Manassas fight, and how I came off with flying colors, victor.

You know a lot of us chaps have been tutored by Mr. Lowell. Well, he took the war fever desperately, and now he's off as chaplain, much to our vexation, for he was such a good, easy soul, we had gay times at school. Now we have a Mr. Marsh, and we don't like him, and we should hate him, only we can't quite get up to that, he's such a gentleman. *He's* his own master, anyhow.

Well, we'd loafed and idled so long that we found it pretty hard to come to terms, — a few of us, at least, for some of the boys are like **lambs**. Well, Hal, and Van, and Court, and Steve, and I, thought we'd try and see how far we could go with the new man without being brought up. So, one day, we came to recitation with never a word of our lesson learned. Mr. Marsh looked us through and through, and then said, —

"How's this, boys?"

"Please, sir," said Van, as soft as silk, "we didn't have time. We never had to get such hard lessons."

"It's time you commenced then. I shall expect the lesson prepared before you go home."

He wasn't one bit cross, but just spoke and looked as much as to say, "I'm master here."

You better believe we growled and scolded well when we met again, on our way home, after having lost our fun at recess, and lost having our own way, too. I felt mutinous enough; but I thought I'd fight this little skirmish with myself, and then I should get my hand in before the pitched battle came on. So I got my lesson, and so did the rest, after a fashion. When we had finished, Mr. Marsh said to us all, but he looked at me, —

"Now I see what you are capable of, I shall be less lenient in future."

That roiled me, — it sounded like a threat, — so I felt all ready to join in with the other boys, who wanted to get up a row. I could n't see exactly where the "leniency" came in. I'd had to eat humble pie, lose my play time, and learn my lesson. So when the boys proposed a general stampede from school hours, next morning, and to trust to luck for the end of the scrape, I thought I'd join. I thought 't would be good fun, too, to see what he 'd do to us, — nothing very dreadful, we thought. I did n't pledge myself, though, and only said he was a mean old thing, and I'd like to plague him. We thought the worst he 'd do would be to give us a flogging, and as that would be a novelty, we 'd like to try it. We agreed to meet in Van's grove at half past eight in the morning, and decide finally about it. When I got home, somehow I thought mother looked sad, and then I thought I should n't like to worry her. I thought I'd think it all over when I went to bed; but I was so sleepy, I could n't, and off I went to sleep in the midst of the *pros* and *cons*. I waked up with a sort of feeling that the *cons* had it. Any way, I did n't get my lesson, and went to the grove, as I promised, and found the other boys thought it was a settled thing, and were making their plans for the day.

"Not so fast, chaps," said I; "I'm on the fence yet, — have n't quite made up my mind to go in for this thing, — don't quite 'see it' yet."

"What a spoony, to back out now!" said Hal. "Been to see little what's-his-name, no-legs, up there, and he would n't let you join the rowdies, eh? or does n't your mother know you 're out?"

"Nonsense!" sneered Van; "he's conscientious scruples, no doubt."

"No," said Court; "he's afraid, — let him go; no cowards train in this company."

This fling settled the question double quick. Before, I'd half made up my mind to join the boys, just for the sake of the scrape, and to see what stuff Mr. Marsh was made of; but when Court said that, I thought of you, and what a rare chance this was to fight the battle; and then I knew I was n't a coward, and I knew the boys knew it, too. Was n't I mad, though! I felt just like a big beer bottle, all working and working inside, and trying to get the stopple out; but something kept it down. If it had come out, wouldn't there have been a burst!

So I kept cool as I could, and just thought it over, — how my mother would feel, what Herbert would say, and how I knew it would be wrong; so I put out my pickets, as you advised, for I knew the battle hadn't come yet, and that I might be taken prisoner after all, and said to Court, stepping back as I spoke, "You are right; I shan't train in this company; whether it is because I am a coward or not, I leave you to judge."

"Here's a pretty go; sneak, traitor, time-server," said one and another.

It was mighty hard work keeping the stopple in then, I tell *you;* but I did, and just gave them a look and turned off, when Court, who was nearest, took hold of me roughly, and said with a wicked oath, "you shan't go till you have given your reasons for this mean conduct."

"Leave me alone then. I thought I should join you at first, but when I came to think of it, I knew it wasn't right."

"Pretty dear, it shan't do what's wrong, shall it; it'll get a whipping if it does," said Court.

"Hurrah boys, here's the greatest farce of the season. Horace Grey turned good boy."

There, I've told you enough, as long as you know how boys talk.

"Any how," said Court, who is a regular bully,

"you shall fight your way out of us, if you want to go and play informer, and curry favor with old redhead."

I said I did n't want to fight then, and they jeered at me again, and looked as if they meant I should at any rate.

At last, Steve, who had been quiet all along, said, "Fair play, boys; you are n't going to fight four to one. Let's make a ring round him, and if he can break through and get over the fence before we catch him, let him go. He's not worth such a fuss."

I did break through between Steve and Van, and was over the fence quick step, you may be sure, and saying, "we 'll settle this another day, boys," was off to school. I was late, and not in the best of trim, and of course missed in my lessons, and had to bear all the penalties; but no questions were asked.

I told mother all about it, and she thought I 'd gained a pretty good victory. I did n't know before 't would be such hard work to fight Horace Grey. But now I 've conquered him once, 't will be easier next time. So you see I 've beaten the enemy, and the enemy has beaten you. I must brag just that little. But I 'm not out of the woods yet, for I don't know as I can keep my temper if the boys are so *aggawatin* again. But I 'll try.

CHAPTER IX.

HORACE GAINS THE VICTORY.

HORACE was right; he was not out of the woods. I will relate to you the rest of his battle, or perhaps I should call it his second engagement with the enemy, for although he described it to Thornton, it was in a very laconic style, having exhausted his writing abilities in his first account.

Mr. Marsh, knew more about the matter than the boys were aware of, for he had been passing through the grove and had heard their conversation on the morning that Horace had resisted the boys. Previous to this he had looked upon him as a boy who would give him a good deal of trouble. He misjudged him, in fact, as almost every one but his mother and St. John, did.

There are few persons who discriminate sufficiently in judging a boy's character, to see the difference between getting into scrapes from a love of fun and an excess of animal spirits, or from depravity and wickedness. As soon as his teacher found that Horace could resist temptation, and conquer his temper, the boy rose at once high in his esteem. He did not abate one jot of the penalties he had incurred by his tardiness, and neglect of lessons, but he treated him with a consideration that Horace felt, and the other boys noticed, at once. It increased their ill-will towards him, and made them resolve to disgrace him if possible.

Mr. Marsh had not called upon Horace to inform against the others, neither had he asked them any questions about the matter. Such a course was to be pursued only in case of necessity, and urgent necessity it must be too. For he knew that the system of informing against each other had a bad effect upon both parties. In this case he had all the information that was needful for him, and he took his measures accordingly.

When the truants appeared in school the day after their voluntary holiday, he took no notice of the matter, but went on with the usual routine of the day. When school was dismissed, however, he bade the delinquents remain, and then, without tempting them to equivocation by questions, told them what he had overheard, and the penalty each one must suffer for his fault.

"I shall also," he said, "report to your parents this affair, and ascertain if I am to be your master, or you mine. In the former case, you will, as I have already told you, remain one hour after school each day, till the time of your absence is made up, learning lessons which I shall give out to you, and making up at home the duties neglected upon that day. I shall also consider you bound as manly boys, and as the sons of gentlemen, to a different course hereafter. Flogging I do not choose to inflict. It is a punishment degrading to him who inflicts, and to him who receives it. In large public schools it doubtless must be resorted to. I shall not resort to it here. If milder measures fail, expulsion shall be my last remedy."

This happened on Friday, and in the afternoon of that day Horace met Van coming over to see him.

"We are to meet in the grove to-morrow, Horace, and talk this matter over," he said, "and make up our minds what to do; and we want you to come too. We think, if we make a great fuss our governors' 'll give old red-head his walking-ticket, and get somebody who 'll not be quite so strict with the sons of gentlemen."

"Be sure and come; nine o'clock's the time."

"For what purpose? *My* mind's made up now."

"Well, to settle old scores then; you promised to some time, when we let you off t'other day. We could have thrashed you as easy as not then. Yes, or no, which is the word?"

"Yes, I'll be on hand."

Van had been very civil thus far, but as he turned to go he said, in a sneering tone, "don't forget."

"Never fear," replied Horace, good-naturedly; my memory is better than you think."

"I must go," he said to himself after Van left him, "I 'spose it would be real mean not to, after what has happened. I'm afraid I shall get hopping mad. Forewarned is forearmed though, and I'll put out my pickets strong all round, and if the enemy catches me, 't wont be without a desperate struggle first."

Accordingly at nine the next morning Horace met the boys at the grove. They received him pleasantly enough, and Court began with, " my constituents have chosen me to express their sentiments for them in a speech." Here he waved his right hand towards the boys and continued, " we think our liberties have been infringed upon, or rather perhaps I should say we think they are to be infringed upon by our new instructor; therefore we deem it advisable to — ahem, take time by the forelock and assert ourselves before we find ourselves in — a — hem — such a fix we can't get out of it. Now our minds are made up, or at least nearly so," he added, as one or two of the boys made a gesture of dissent. "You see here is the case; we are the sons of rich men, aristocrats; consequently, we are not to be treated like the sons of men in the lower walks of life. Coercion (that's the crack word now) 'll do for *them*, never for *us*. Our fathers don't wish us to be coerced into study. They believe it will be far more politic if the powers that be (otherwise, old red-head) yield a little, compromise a little; at least we believe it and of course our fathers are dutiful enough to agree with us. To be sure, red-head hasn't done anything very bad yet, only to require us to get our lessons and obey him. But it is plain he is prepared to be a terrible tyrant if once he gets firm hold of the reins of government. He doesn't know how to manage *us;* as how should he, a Connecticut yankee, son or nephew at least to a tin pedler or wooden nutmeg dealer. I don't know what he is, but I infer it, and our class are quick at inferences. So the long and short of it is, friends, we intend to secede, and either govern ourselves or choose a teacher who will respect our feelings and prejudices. **We have with us an** old and long-cherished institution, one **dear as life** to all our hearts; **that of** having our **own way,** and we cannot, no, we will not, give it up; better far to die a thousand deaths than thus ignobly **yield.** My brothers, my constituents, I hope and I believe, we are of one mind upon this subject. Some great man has said a — a — divided we, — no that is not it. United we stand, divided we fall. Friends, countrymen, lovers, am I right, — are we united? I see but one dissentient face."

"I hear a sound you cannot hear, I see a sight you cannot see. So please stop, Master Courtland Templeton; your constituents respond to your very eloquent and original address, and pronounce it a very nice hash from the Sunny South, Yankeedom, and Rome. We were all convinced before you began and are 'more so' now; even Master Horace Grey, whilom so near becoming a traitor is all right, and goes in for secession strong. I propose three cheers and a tiger for our representative's thrilling and patriotic address."

The above interruption was made by Van, who had long been fidgetting under Court's protracted speech. Three cheers and a tiger were given, and then there was a pause, an evident waiting for Horace.

He straightened himself up from a leaning posture against a tree, looked around with a half smile, and said, "As quotation is the order of the day I begin with

'He who is convinced against his will,
Holds to the same opinion still."

"I bow to the eloquence and unanswerable arguments of Master Templeton, but as I find myself in that singular predicament of being at once party and leader, constituent and speaker, my words in reply shall be few.

"Briefly, then, I have decided not to secede, but to submit to coercion, or in other words to obey Mr. Marsh's rules and conform to his wishes, at least until he proves himself a tyrant. As for the notion some of you entertain that I was pledged to join you the other day, it is a mistake. I told you I'd think about it. I did think about it, and I thought I would n't. I have nothing more to say."

"But by —" (and here Hal, for he it was who had started forward when Horace finished, swore a wicked oath), "*we* have a great deal more to say about it. If you do not join us we will be revenged upon you in one way or another. War it shall be between us now and forever. If you join these sneaking goody fellows, who will do anything to curry favor, we will have nothing more to do with you, in school or out, *except*," he added, maliciously, " to take our revenge on you; and we shall consider you as a mean, cowardly chap."

"Can't help it if you do; my mind is made up; and I've as good a right to take my way as you yours. It takes two sides to make a quarrel, and I've none with you. I don't wish to lose your friendship, but I can bear even that in a good cause."

"Let it go home to its own mammy and its saint of a brother, and be fed on sugar-plums, and be cosseted for being good, and then it shall go to its little pretty playmate, and make dolls and jackstraws, it shall," said Van, in his most sneering tones.

Ridicule is a powerful weapon, and boys and girls are particularly susceptible to it, not having learned that, which is a hard lesson for any to learn, — to be indifferent to the laugh it occasions.

Horace heard the other boys laugh, all but Steve, and he found now was his hour of danger, and the need he had of the picket guard he had stationed around his camp. Do you wish to know what this guard was?

Thoughts of the promise he had made his brother Thornton, of his mother, and of what was right and just. These thoughts secured him from quite falling into the enemy's power. The fling about dolls and jackstraws irritated him exceedingly. He had employed some leisure rainy days in helping Herbert paint a military company designed for a fair to be held by some little girls in the neighborhood, in behalf of the soldiers, and also in whittling out jackstraws for the same purpose. The boys had laughed at him at the time, called him a Miss Nancy and a Yankee, and advised him to open a toy-shop; but he had laughed it off, and given them back, as he said, as good as they sent.

He was in no mood for laughing now. He was *very* angry, — what boys call mad, in fact, — and it was hard fighting. The enemy beset him before and behind, and he could with a hearty good-will have pitched (I use the phrase that expresses his feeling) into Van then and there, and stopped his taunts about his mother and Herbert. He did not yield, however. He gained a great victory, — a victory it was, although he was angry, for he kept back the expression of his feelings. And while he was thus manfully fighting his battle, lo! a new ally appeared in the person of Steve Harwood. He stepped forward and said, —

"It's a mighty poor cause that needs ridicule to uphold it. I join Horace now."

Were n't the three boys left vexed enough! To use one of their own favorite expressions, "you'd better believe" they were, not only vexed and angry, but mad, — raging like wild creatures. All the epithets at command of Van were freely bestowed upon first Horace, and then Steve; and Van's vocabulary of "naughty words" was neither small nor choice. It was bad enough for Horace to have deserted them, — Horace, whose father was a rich and influential man in the neighborhood, — but that was trifling to Steve's loss to their side. Steve was the oldest of them all, between fifteen and sixteen, and his father was quite the nabob of the place; and he, Steve, had unlimited powers at home, — so, at least, the boys thought, — and upon his influence they had reckoned to carry out their foolish scheme. Without him, they saw only discomfiture and final submission.

"Come on, then, cowards and deserters, and fight it out!" roared Hal.

"No," said Steve, calmly, "we'll not fight. Horace is in the right; but, for all that, as I hate to study, I dare say I should have kept with you if you had n't used unfair weapons. I think the meanness and cowardice comes in where you twit a boy about his mother and his kindness to a poor deformed fellow. That's my opinion, and you can take it free gratis, and make the most of it. I think, too," he added, changing his tone, "the best thing you can do is to let this rest, and come to school Monday in an orderly fashion. Come, Horace. Good morning, boys, and a better mind to you when we meet again."

The immediate result of this affair was a request on the part of the fathers of the refractory boys that Mr. Marsh should remain, promising good behavior on behalf of their sons for the future.

When the boys met at school the following Monday, the three would-be seceders were very civil, and apparently on friendly terms with the others.

"A violent storm soon blown over," said Horace to Steve.

"Humph! I've heard of storms blowing over, and coming up again in another quarter of the heavens. They have n't done with us yet; but I'm not afraid. As for you, Horace, you did well, and made me feel ashamed of myself."

CHAPTER X.

THORNTON LEARNS BY EXPERIENCE THE TRUTH OF AN OLD PROVERB.

I TOLD you, at the beginning of this story, that it would not be a connected history of a soldier's life in the army, but a series of sketches and incidents, illustrative of the different phases of his experience, and of the leading idea of the book. Therefore, I now make a long leap, from the time of Thornton's first bloody and fearful battle, to a period of comparative rest and "masterly inactivity."

January, '62. Well, Horace, my young fighter, we've been having a pretty queer muddle of an experience since I last journalized for your benefit, — a mingling of the serious and comic, — out of which I leave you to gather hints to aid and fun to amuse you.

A pretty *serious* matter it was to our company, a week ago, when, about four in the morning, we were tumbled out of our tents, with the order to fall in, stumbling over each other and every tumble-over-able article near, and sent off a mile in pursuit of a small body of Rebels, who were quietly waiting for the morning light to do us some mischief, — so, at least, the report had come to us. Of course, they did n't mean a serious attack, but had their eye upon some supplies they thought were in an available position for a raid.

Our captain, Ned Howe, of whom I spoke as belonging to our set in the city, led us a pretty wild-goose chase. Under the influence of that subtle enemy which steals away the brains, he mistook his orders, and marched us off into a morass, after floundering through which, we brought up square against a wood too thick to be a hiding-place for any but Lilliputian warriors, and were ordered to fire; which we did in the dim light of the waning moon, and received for response the echo of our own firearms, followed by curses loud and deep from our own men upon the discovery that the enemy was n't "thar."

It was some time before Captain Howe recovered his wits enough to be made to realize his blunder; and when he did, he swore roundly that the —— Rebels had given him the slip, and gone round 't other way!

We returned to camp, angry and mortified, minus a good round of ammunition, and all our patience, and plus a liberal coating of mud, and aching limbs.

Ned was *not* discharged, — O, no! The matter was hushed up in some remarkable manner; and, because he was high in office, and had influential friends, he was allowed to remain and lead his men into the cannon's mouth, or, still more trying to us, into ridiculous and shameful positions.

Meantime, while we had marched through the swamp and back again, another company, ordered out to support us, had **taken the right** direction, bagged the enemy mostly, and were quietly resting on their laurels when we got back.

Our fellow-soldiers twitted us for a time with sly allusions to *safe* mistakes, verdant groves, and Virginia mud, till they were coolly informed 't was hardly prudent to make game of us for one man's sin.

Now, Horace, I must say a few words to you about the mischief done, disgrace and **ruin** wrought, by that one vice, intemperance.

The privates, of course, can't get liquor, except in some rare cases of smuggling, and private barter with friendly Rebs. The officers can, and do. So our country, engaged in a war which should check all the lower vices, and call out every noble feeling, presents to the world the spectacle of brave, self-sacrificing men led to the front of battle by officers who have not yet learned to control their appetites, and who, under the dominion of intemperance, have caused the destruction of their subordinates. I know very many of our officers are as noble and true men in every respect as the world ever saw, — brave, self-sacrificing, unflinching, masters of themselves and their soldiers; but there are all too many who are the reverse of all this, — cowards, because too timid to resist evil desires; selfish, because forgetful of their great responsibilities; vacillating, because their heads are dizzy and bewildered with their potations.

Touch not, taste not, handle not the vile poison; abjure it forever, now while you are young, if you would be a man and not a brute. Some of the officers who are intemperate abstain from the immoderate use of liquor till the battle is over, and then get beastly drunk. Coarse language, you will say, as applied to gentlemen.(?) No language is coarse enough to express the vileness of the habit, none strong enough to portray the mischief its indulgence causes.

Imagine, though I loathe the thought of describing such a scene to you, imagine one of our brave officers, who in battle has had the look and bearing almost of a God among men, so royally did he bear upon his face the image and daring of a hero, imagine him lying upon the floor of his tent, either a senseless brute, too steeped in liquor to be conscious of anything, or looking a very baboon, with his leering visage, his thick speech, or senseless jargon. A brute, did I say? I ask pardon of the brute creation for the insult. Look at his horse, and see how far nobler an animal he is of the two! Again, I say to you touch not, taste not, handle not the vile stuff. The temptation to indulge is strong for one who has the appetite, either before or after battle, either as a help to greater courage, or as a relief from weariness and exhaustion. But enough of this. If Ned Howe does n't lead himself and us into trouble before he's done with us, I shall be glad to prove a false prophet, — but he has taken a good many downward steps since we left home. In the army, if never before in this life, one realizes the force of the petition, lead us not into temptation.

Should you like to have an account of one of our foraging expeditions? Yes, I know that will be something after your own heart. You may not be surprised to hear that we have not met with the far-famed Virginia hospitality, and hence that we have been under **the** necessity of taking the matter **into** our own hands, and supply ourselves, with the permission of our superior officers, of course. The craving for fresh meat and soft bread becomes pretty strong **after** a long diet on salt horse (as some of our men disrespectfully call the beef), and hard tack, and when these latter articles become scarce, it is quite useless to forbid the men from taking what they can find from their enemies. This is the case now, — rain and mud, — mud, such as you, in your lofty perch on the Hudson, never dreamed of, have delayed the arrival of our supplies, and permission is given a certain number of men, under the command of a corporal, to go forth and see what they can find, under restrictions, however, not to use needless violence, or inflict wanton injury upon anything, or interfere with those who have a Government protection. Something is said, too, about our not being Goths and Vandals, if we have the reputation of being so; and having respectfully received orders, and listened to advice, we decorously march out of camp, and out of sight of camp. Holdfast, Pat, Brag, myself, and half a dozen others, under command of Corporal Trim.

Decorously, while in sight of camp, but double quick, each at his own pace of that measure, too, when the woods are between us and our officers.

"Hoorah for fresh vittles, and good luck to that same boy that finds the biggest spoil. An its meself that'll rin off wid the first pig I lay me hands on," said Pat.

"Be sure and git a good grip on the cretur, Pat; them's pesky slippery, them air," said Holdfast.

"And be sure that the old woman don't give you a hot shower-bath while you're seizing her pig," said Brag. "I've heard of such retaliation."

"It's along of yer ignorance," retorted Pat; "ye suppose I can't manage any ould wooman of em all. Yer niver saw my ould wooman, an the way I kape her straight, or yer would n't be after misdoubting me this way. Was n't she that spiteful and quarrelsome loike, that she kept the whole neighborhood in an uproor, and niver would live out to sarvice at all; an' there was talk of sending her to the House of Corriction, an' I thought that was shame for her when she was the child of my fourth cousin removed, in the ould counthry, an' so I jes married her, and be me faith and St. Patrick, she's as quite as a lamb sence."

"Waal, I call that ar reel grit," said Holdfast. "I've faced many a wild cretur in the backwoods to hum, but a cantankerous woman's beyond me. I ain't fraid of nothin' else."

These words, with the honest look of admiration Holdfast bestowed upon Pat, set us all into a roar.

"Steady there, boys," said Corporal Trim, who was never known to be anything but steady himself, whatever he was about. "Here's one place I've had my eye on for some time."

We were in sight of one of those dilapidated, miserable-looking houses so common in Virginia, but still dignified (?) by still more wretched-looking negro cabins around. Open-mouthed negro children stared at us, and upon our near approach ran off to report our arrival.

A loud knock of Corporal Trim's brought to the door a lean, sallow-visaged woman, who planted herself in our way, with arms akimbo. To a civil demand for food she answered gruffly, "Reckon you'll have to help yourselves; reckon 'taint my business to feed Abe Lincoln's armies."

"Thank you, marm," said Corporal Trim, with his most polite bow, " that's all we want, the liberty to help ourselves. We did n't know as you'd like to have us tramping over your clean floors. Sorry to trouble you, marm, but this is one of the chances of war."

"None of your soft sawder to me; git what you kin and be off with you; hope it'll choke every —— Yankee of you."

"I pray, marm, don't be so hard-hearted, — step along boys, steady there."

Nothing loath we obeyed; and visited kitchen larder and cellar, and found — several well-picked ham bones, a little cold corn bread, and a little corn meal.

Holdfast, who had petitioned for leave to search out of doors, examined the smoke-house with like want of success.

Returning to the kitchen, our Corporal politely said, "Pray what do you live upon, marm?"

"Anything we kin pick up," was the sullen answer.

"Small pickens here," said Holdfast.

"If you'll allow me, marm," said Corporal Trim, stepping towards a door against which the woman leaned half-defiantly, half-carelessly.

"It's nothin' but a bedroom, and my darter's mighty sick thar. You would n't be so barbarous's t' sturb her!"

Now, it had struck me that a frowsy head and red face that we caught a glimpse of at the window as we came up, had nowhere been visible; and probably the same idea had occurred to our Corporal, for he persisted in passing the woman, and opening the door. At first sight nothing met our view but a most uncomfortable, untidy-looking room, with heaps of bedclothes upon the bed, and a frowsy head just visible.

"Bless me, marm, what a high fever your daughter's in! I served my time, at home, in a 'pothecary shop; maybe I could prescribe for her," said Trim, as a farther entrance into the room revealed the red face of the invalid.

"None of your prescribin's for us; we don't take pisins with our eyes open. Ef you're convinced the gal's sick, jest step out, with your men, ef you've any decency left!"

"Yes, marm, quite convinced," said Trim, disarranging some of the bedclothes, and bringing to view some sacks of meal, and pointing significantly under the bed. We did n't wait for farther permission, but dragged out a couple of boxes, in which we found a good store of bacon, and a small firkin containing eggs.

Corporal Trim allowed us to take but half of the spoils, and most politely bade the woman good morning. Her rage was excessive. No French fish wife could ever have exceeded her in the license she gave her tongue. Her daughter, too, recovered sufficiently to join her mother in abuse of us, our country, our Government, and our President.

"Whew!" said Trim, when once more in the open air, "it's kind of stifled in there. I say, boys, isn't it remarkable that there should be eggs, and no signs of chickens or hens about? Hallo! there's a queer noise. What *are* you sitting on, youngster?"

This was addressed to a boy, a miniature likeness of the fever-stricken daughter of the house, who sat perched upon the top of a reversed hogshead in one corner of the yard, from whence, despite a vigorous whistling on his part, proceeded strange sounds.

The boy was speedily dismounted from his perch, and the hogshead as speedily turned over; and then commenced a regular skedaddle therefrom of hens, roosters, and chickens.

"Easy, boys; don't take many. They deserve a reward for their ingenuity; and there's a prime lot of poultry and live stock on the next place we're going to," said Trim.

Rather unwillingly we obeyed, thinking of the old proverb, "A bird in hand is worth two in the bush," — the truth of which we were doomed to prove.

"Now, boys," said Trim, as we marched off with our spoils, "a little more quiet this time. It isn't worth while to give these civil people the trouble to hide away their stores, — best not to give notice."

Our next adventure was in striking contrast to the first. True, the negro children stared as before, but did not run away; and the woman who opened the door to us, after growling out a few indistinct words, to which we paid no heed, contented herself with scowling upon and watching us narrowly. I thought she was even making a list of the articles we took; and we had a harvest here, — corn, meal, bacon, eggs, vegetables, poultry, and live stock in abundance, we found; and as there seemed plenty, we helped ourselves generously. Pat secured his pig, and the rest of us took turkeys and chickens freely; and, finally, when we were so loaded we could n't take any more, we left, thanking our frowning hostess for her liberal contribution to our wants. To our surprise, she frowned no longer, but gave us a grin which we were at a loss to interpret; for it was of that nature that did n't indicate much good will. The interpretation came soon enough, however.

Well, we had a jolly, if a heavy, march home to the camp; and our mouths watered as we revelled in luxuries in imagination, and had our "chicken fixins" prepared to our taste. Chickens are rather a luxury at home, but you can't tell how high they loom up in that list after salt beef, varied with salt beef, week in and week out. So we must not be set down as gluttons if "chicken fixins" was still the burden of our song.

But, alas! alas! there's many a slip between the cup and lip. Pride must have a fall, and so did our elation; for we had no sooner arrived at camp, told our tale most triumphantly, and described the location of the two plantations we had visited, than we were coolly informed that the one we last visited had a Government protection!

"Why in —— did n't the hag show it, then?" said Corporal Trim, fairly enraged out of his propriety.

"Because you did n't ask for it, probably; though she says she did tell you so, and you took no notice of her."

"She says!" said Corporal Trim, aghast; "is the woman a witch?"

"No, only a keen woman. She took a list of the articles you appropriated, and as soon as you were out of sight, despatched a fleet messenger to camp. The lad is half-way home now."

"What's to be done?"

"Return everything that is not injured, pay for what is, out of your own pockets, and make an apology,—at least, tell the woman you did n't know she had a protection."

"She's as arrant a Rebel as ever wore petticoats," said Trim.

"No matter," said our superior officer; "her husband's an Unionist, and she has a protection."

"If we must, we must, I s'pose," said our discomfited leader. "*That's* what her infernal grin meant!"

I can't dwell much upon our return to the abode of plenty, nor its results. This time we felt we were fair game to the rest of the company, and so bravely joined in the laugh; and by unanimous vote, called our camp, "Camp Chicken Fixins."

I think I have verified to you the truth of the old proverb, "There's many a slip between the cup and the lip."

CHAPTER XI.

INSIDIOUS FOES.

WEEKS passed, and nothing occurred on the part of the intended seceders to confirm Steve's prophecy that "they hadn't done with them yet." On the contrary, they were pleasant and conciliating in their demeanor, and maintained a better rank in school than ever before. Mr. Marsh treated them with kindness and consideration. Horace said, laughingly, to Steve, one day, —

"It takes a long time for your storm to come up. Guess we've weathered this gale, anyhow."

Steve shook his head. *He* knew the boys, Hal and Van, at least, to be resentful and vindictive, and Court was easily led by the others. But he didn't give himself much trouble about the matter. He had no fears on his own part, and he hardly saw how they could injure Horace. The affair had done Steve a great deal of good. It had roused him from his indolence; and the wish to retrieve his character with Mr. Marsh had induced greater faithfulness in his studies. This brought with it its own reward; and his lessons, hitherto a task, became a pleasure;

and he was now, what he had always been capable of being, one of the best scholars in the school. So the slight circumstance of his taking the part of Horace against the other boys, had results for him which affected his whole future course in life.

But to return to our home soldier. His case was like that of many an older and more experienced one. A great victory had made him self-confident, and careless of more insignificant enemies. These were more numerous than he was aware of. Because they did not come to him roaring and raging, and compelling him to do battle, or yield at once, as in his former experience, he slackened in his watchfulness, and neglected to keep his pickets well posted. He did not recall the stirring counsel of the hymn,—

> "Awake, my soul! lift up thine eyes,
> See where thy foes against thee rise,—
> In long array, a numerous host,—
> Awake, my soul! or thou art lost!"

Neither did he remember that,—

> "The meanest foe of all the train
> Has thousands and ten thousands slain."

No; he wrote to Thornton, in a most self-congratulatory manner, that one good fight was the best thing in the world for a fellow, and added, "I'm afraid I sha n't be able to keep up with you in gallant exploits, for one bout with the enemy has beaten him."

And all this time Horace was losing ground in scholarship and in strict principle!

Naturally a bright boy, he could easily maintain a good rank in school with ordinary attention to his studies; but he was so fond of play and out of door exercise, that he was very apt to neglect study out of school, for amusement. Faithful scholarship required that the boys should give some of their time at home to their lessons, although there was still abundance left for recreation. Of course, he belonged to a military company, the Highland Zouaves by name, for all boys from six years upwards took the military fever. Some took it so severely that playing soldier ended in real soldiership, a little later; others took it so lightly that it ended with the gloss of their new uniforms, and if not in literal, at least metaphorical smoke.

But Horace, of course, with his military aspirations, had the fever severely, with all its most violent symptoms, and was so thoroughly imbued with it, that everything for a time was done *en militaire*. His school satchel was slung like a knapsack upon his back; Cæsar was called upon to enact the enemy, and receive imaginary charges in front, and surprises in the rear; was humiliated by being taken prisoner, or astounded by the vociferous imprecations bestowed upon him, if he turned tail and fled. The family were greeted with military salutes; his mother's nicely-cooked viands were designated as salt horse, and hard tack, and once or twice he made imaginary bayonet charges, with the carving knife, at the sirloin, till peremptorily forbidden to bring the camp to the dinner-table.

With this fascination upon him, of course, all his leisure time, and much that was not lawfully such, was spent in camp, drilling, or in marching, camping out, &c. And this was not all, nor the worst. He spent more time in lounging about, and talking over their last performances, and planning something new for the next, than in the real duties of camp life; and then his lessons were — where? All boys with like propensities can tell me.

He belonged, also, to a boat club; and the river side was another favorite resort of his, where he would rock idly in one of the boats, talking with the man who had charge of them, or with some companion as careless as himself, and as averse to indoor pursuits.

One day his mother remonstrated with him upon these habits, and his evident neglect of his studies.

"A boy must have some time to play, mother. It's enough to be cooped up in school from nine till two, without spending any more time studying. My opinion is, mother, that the house was never intended for boys to live in, — only to eat and sleep in."

"So it seems you think," replied his mother, gently; "but, unfortunately for you, neither your father nor I hold to the same opinion. A boy has duties, as well as pleasures. I just came from Mrs. Harwood's. When I went there, an hour ago, Steve was sitting on the piazza, studying his lesson. 'Don't you go out to-day with the Zouaves, Steve?' I asked. 'O yes, ma'am,' he answered; 'we've had a drill, and a march, and it was all over half an hour ago.' I came home to find you just coming up the avenue. Play while you play, Horace, and work when you work; that's a good motto for you."

"I only stopped to talk over a plan for one of our marches, with Van."

"No special harm in that, to be sure, if you had no lessons to learn at home, or any other duty to attend to; although one great objection I have to these lounging chats is, that, though boys may begin with their boat club, the affairs of their company, their last game, whatever it may be, they often end in conversation, or, I should say, talk, less innocent. Is it not so?"

"Sometimes I suppose it is, with bad boys."

"And with boys not altogether what you'd call bad. When boys are out together, I believe in *action*, doing something. Let them come home to rest and talk, and bring their companions with them."

"Can't a boy ever talk to another except in the house?"

"Did I say they could n't, Horace? I am only speaking of those pernicious, loitering chats, when often boys are needed at home for some duty, or if they are not, they ought to be there. Besides, I think some of your home pleasures not so very much restricted to the house; for instance, riding Whitefoot to accompany Margaret, walks with your mother, work in your garden, and exercise in the gymnasium."

"Well, please may n't I go out and have a race with Cæsar? Guess I could n't remember any more good advice now."

"Yes," said his mother, smiling, "presently, if you will listen to one more suggestion. The time spent in loitering *might* save rebukes, and dismissals from the table for rough hair and dirty hands, and might give a boy time to put away his possessions, and hang up his cap."

"Please don't say any more now,—I'm off!"

You may be very sure the boys who were anxious to cause Horace's disgrace, took advantage of this failing. There was always some pretext or other for delay after the others had gone home from drill, or boating; and if once they had detained Horace, he was safe in their hands for a definite or indefinite space of time, as the case might be, according to their wishes.

The reward of all this negligence was the, to Horace, astounding address of Mr. Marsh to him, one day:—

"Horace Grey, are you aware how your report stands?"

The severe tone in which this question was asked, startled Horace, and he answered, meekly, —

"No, sir."

"I am, unfortunately for you. You have a lower average than any boy in school, with, perhaps, two exceptions. This, for a boy of good abilities, good health, and good home influence, is unpardonable. Your carelessness and neglect have been so apparent to the whole school, that I have no hesitation in thus publicly reprimanding you. See to it that your course is changed. The term is nearly half over, but you can still retrieve your character, if you will. All that you need is a little less time spent in play and idling, and a little more devoted to study.

"And now, boys," Mr. Marsh continued, "I have a proposal of general interest to make. You have most of you made good progress in drawing and writing. I propose that you should outline a map of the United States, filling up with accuracy and marking special war localities, the District of Columbia, Maryland, and Virginia. The design, as you doubtless understand, is to fix in your minds interesting facts and situations relating to the war. I shall wish you, at some future time, to go on and fill up the remainder of the map. You cannot do this without work, nor without making some sacrifice of your amusements; but if you manage with system, I believe it will not be an alarming one. To the one who, in the opinion of six impartial judges, succeeds the best, I will with pleasure give — my cordial approbation and — a copy of Irving's Life of Washington. Those of you who approve my proposal will signify it by saying ' Ay.'"

A deafening shout of ayes rang through the schoolroom.

"Those who disapprove, — and by disapproval I mean indifference, as well as decided objection, — will signify it by saying ' No.'"

A faint no was heard from one of the idlers of the school, — one, moreover, who never seemed able to draw a straight line. At this sound, the other boys laughed.

Mr. Marsh looked reprovingly at them, and said:

"Bravely done, George Lee! You have been honest, as well as brave, and I count those two great virtues. Many boys, perhaps some among those who have just laughed at your moral courage, would have joined the majority, conscious all the while they had neither the wish nor the ability to do as I desire. Again I say, bravely done, and I honor you for it."

"Now's your time, Horace," said Steve. "You draw better than most of us, and you'll be sure to succeed if you will only be careful."

"Now's *our* time," said Van to Hal. "We'll start something that'll keep him from having much time to draw."

"I don't know as those dodges'll work any longer.

If old Marsh had n't spoken out just yet to him, we could have managed it all right."

"Pooh! I'll risk it yet. If he gets the prize, I'll let him alone in future, as too sharp for us. But get the prize he never shall. If fair means don't succeed, I'll use foul."

"What do you call fair means?"

"O, enticing him away to play, and talk, and that sort of thing. There's other means can be used. I've waited too long now to pay off that old score, —— him. He's mistaken if he thinks I've forgotten. No, no; I never forget, and I'll pay him double for himself and Steve, too. I dare n't meddle with Steve; besides, it was all *his* fault."

Mortified and half-repentant, Horace walked slowly home, thinking over the last few weeks, and realizing fully that it would have been far better if he had listened more heedfully to his mother's advice. Like many boys, pretty good boys, too, in the main, he had an idea that a woman could n't be supposed to understand a boy's needs, and that even an affectionate mother might at times be unreasonable in her requirements. Now he had proved the truth of her words; and gladly would he have recalled the hours worse than wasted, when he should have been attending to his studies. He resolved, however, upon a different course in future, and determined to try for the prize, — not that he cared very much for the books, but he knew success would gratify his parents, and help to reinstate him in Mr. Marsh's good opinion.

He stopped to see Herbert Vane, and told him of his intention to try and get the prize Mr. Marsh had offered. He couldn't quite make up his mind to tell him of his mortification and disgrace, but said —

"Marsh was cross as a bear to-day, and gave me a sitting down because I don't pore over my books all the time. I shall be glad when I get out of school, — I hate it."

Herbert saw that the less he said to Horace about study, the better, in his present mood; so he laughed, and answered —

"That'll do very well for you to *say*, and I know how much it means. About this map, if you'll bring your materials here and draw, I'll help you with my suggestions, and you will be quiet in my room. Only, Horace, I would fix upon some time to come every day, and always come at that hour, unless something very important prevents. If you'll persevere, I guess your chance is as good as any other boy's."

Horace agreed to this plan, and it was decided as drill didn't commence till five o'clock, now that the days were so long, that he should come to Herbert between four and five.

On his way home, he met Court, who said to him, "Too bad in old Marsh to come down upon you so to-day. We're all agreed that 't was real shabby in him, just for a few mistakes. He's partial, too. Steve's the favorite, and nobody else has a chance for his favor. I hate partiality."

"O, I don't think he's partial," said Horace, thoughtfully; "at least, I never did think so; I dare say I deserved all he said."

"Well, if you'll think a little more about it, you'll see he is. Every boy in school thinks so but you, and we fellows are real mad at him on your account. You did us a deal of good that time you kept us out of that scrape you know, and we don't forget it. I hope you don't owe us any grudge, do you? You see we were so mad we did n't know what we were doing."

"Grudge, no indeed," said Horace, looking surprised, for this was the first allusion that had ever been made to the affair. "How could you think I did."

"Oh, nothing in particular, only you seem shy of us, and some boys are so spiteful they never forget anything. I'm right glad you're all *right* though, and Van means to show his good will, by not trying for the prize. He's sure to succeed if he did, he's such a master hand at drawing."

"He's very kind, but I think each boy better do the best he can."

"Oh, he'll do well enough, but then he won't make any great effort. He says he owes you a good turn, and if you succeed in this, it'll set you all right with old Marsh."

For nearly a week after this, Horace persevered

not only in attending to his lessons, but in going regularly to draw at Mr. Vane's, and neither Hal, Van, nor Court, tried to delay him, but on the contrary sometimes gave him a friendly reminder that it was time for him to be going home when he seemed inclined to linger after drill or boating. At the expiration of that time however, they changed their tactics, as will be seen.

"What time do you go to draw Hor," asked Hal, as the boys were going home from school.

"About four o'clock."

"Well, Van wants to consult with you about a plan he has for capturing Fort Dunbar. He means to scale the walls and plant the Union Flag on the highest battlement. He don't want to tell any of the boys but you, till the day comes, for fear they'll let the cat out of the bag, and the enemy'll be prepared for us. He says he wants your advice, you're so daring and spunky. Meet us at the water's edge just below Fort Dunbar, about half past three. That'll not interfere with your drawing. Will you?"

"That's a jolly plan; meet you to be sure I will; it's only going without my dessert, and that's nothing. I've been hoping we should have some sport, and not do all our fighting in such a tame way."

"Well, be sure and be on hand; half past three's the time."

Punctually to the hour Horace was at the spot named.

Hal and Court were there, but not Van.

"Hallo, boys," shouted Horace, "where's the Captain?"

"As bad luck would have it his father had company to dine, and Van said he wouldn't let him off before dessert, and of course dinner would be a little later than usual. But he'll be here before five, and we shall only have to hurry up our talk, answered Hal.

Four o'clock came though, and no Van, and Horace had just decided to go back, when he came hurrying towards them.

"It's too bad, Horace, but I couldn't help it. Here's a little pen-and-ink sketch I've made of the fort, and my plan. See what you think of it."

Horace took the sketch and expressed his approbation, making, however a suggestion or two, to which Van assented cordially, and which Hal opposed vehemently, and Court timidly.

"I shall follow Horace's advice; he's an eye to see things right, boys; so you needn't take offence."

"Of course not," said Hal; "only I think you are making a mistake."

He then proceeded to urge his objections still more decidedly, and time passed rapidly, till Van pulled out his watch and exclaimed, —

"Bless me, it's quarter to five, and there's barely time to get ready to drill. It don't matter for us, but you wanted to go to Mr. Vane's, didn't you, Horace? By the way, how do you get along with the map?"

"Finely. I've made a good beginning; the outline is nearly done."

"Oh, well, then an afternoon's work lost don't signify. 'Well begun, is half done,' you know. Let me see your map when you've finished the outline, will you? I sha n't copy it," he added, with a laugh, as Horace hesitated. "I only want to see how it's done; and we're allowed to make suggestions to each other, you know. You're not too proud to be advised, are you?"

"No, — O no," said Horace; "only, — perhaps, — I thought — "

"O, never mind your reasons; it's no consequence at all;" and Van put away his sketch, took up his cap, and with a pleasant nod hurried off.

"He's a trump," said Hal. "Most any boy would have been mad to have had such an offer treated so coldly."

Horace thought he was a trump, too, and determined he would bring him his map. "'T would be real mean not to," he thought; "and I despise mean things."

Fort Dunbar was a precipitous rock, rising some thirty or forty feet from the river side, almost perpendicularly for about twenty-five feet, then gradually shelving backwards, and terminating in a thick wood. On the shelving part grew a few shrubs and stunted trees, and there were also rough projections of rock. Boys had scaled it in the spirit of adventure, but it was considered a daring feat.

The Highland Zouaves had early in their campaign called it Fort Dunbar, had pretended to regard it as inaccessible, and had talked a great deal about the enemy entrenched in his fortress, and discussed plans for bringing him down to the river side. They had been so earnest in the matter, that one little boy, the youngest of the company, really believed an enemy was there, and inquired if he wore the grey uniform of the Rebels.

CHAPTER XII.

THE SPIDER AND THE FLY.

"HALLO, Court, what's this?" "Boys are forbidden to trespass on these grounds," said Horace to Court one day, as they were passing near a thick wood, and the above notice in staring capital letters greeted their eyes.

"It seems pretty plain to *me* what it is; nothing more nor less than old Skin Flint's notice. That's old Thacher, you knew; whoever heard of a man's forbidding boys to go through a wood before?"

"Van and Hal went through t'other night, just to spite the old fellow, who was spying about. They've got dogs there now, and it is n't quite such fun to risk them. But Van vows he'll play him a trick yet. You know he means—"

"What," said Horace, "means what?"

"Oh, nothing; I was only going to tell about the old man, how cross he is; and how he won't have anything to do with the neighbors, and how surly he is to Van's father. The estates join, you know."

"Yes, I know. I heard father talking about him

the other day; and though he said he should n't do such a thing, yet a man had a perfect right to shut up his woods if he pleased. He told me on no account to go near them; so now I can't join in any trick, and I'm real sorry, for I should like to right well. I hate mean, small people; and if it is n't mean to shut up a wood like a private park, I should like to know what is."

"What will Van do?"

"Oh, I don't know; not much I guess."

"By the way, I was just going after him. Do you know if he's at home?"

"Yes, he just went up the avenue as I came along. Step quick and you'll find him. Special business, eh?"

"No, nothing very special," said Horace, looking confused. A few moments later, and he found Van upon his father's piazza, and taking out his map, said, "I brought you this to look at. I don't know what made me so surly the other day."

"Oh, never mind, 't was natural enough." So saying, Van took the map, examined it carefully, praised the execution, made one or two trifling suggestions, and added, "I've got a splendid map of the seat of war, and you shall see it when you come to fill yours up; but don't tell any of the other fellows. I don't care to help them, or give them my chance."

"But I don't want you to give up trying, for me; it is n't right.

"Pooh, what do I care for old Marsh's opinion, or the book either?"

"I don't care for the books."

"Just so, of course you don't; but naturally you want to show Marsh that you can be careful and persevering. I should I know, out of spite, to prove he was mistaken, if nothing more. Come in a minute and look at my map before you go. I'll tell you in confidence that I mean to take the company up Brice Hill some day on a march. They're a lazy set, the most part of them, and I'll give 'em a tramp. We'll go before and reconnoitre some day, and pick out the worst path we can find. I guess they'll think the enemy's upon them in earnest before they get home again. Let's go to-morrow, will you?"

"What time?"

"Before drill. It's only one afternoon, and you're ahead of all the boys, so you've nothing to fear about your map; here's the one I told you of; is n't it stunning?"

"That's so," said Horace, "splendid and first-rate, too. That'll help me ever so much; it is larger and more complete than the one my father has."

As Horace left the avenue, he met Hal coming in.

"I say Van's a real trump, is n't he?" was his greeting to Hal.

"To be sure; he's worth two of plodding Steve. Steve's well enough; but there's no adventure or spirit in him; none of your Miss Nancy's for me.

I tell *you* we boys are getting jealous of your favor with the Captain."

Horace smiled and passed on; and as the two chief conspirators met, they exchanged significant looks, and then laughed heartily.

"What a guy he is," said Van, contemptuously.

"Yes, for a bold, brave boy as he is, and no mistake, he certainly is the most easily duped of any chap I ever saw," replied Hal. "He really believes you are as much interested for him as you pretend. He just told me you were a trump."

"I *am* interested for him, as he shall see to his cost. No boy ever crosses me without paying for it. I've got him now in my net as safe as the spider had the fly."

"You better caution Court a little, or he'll betray some of your schemes; and if you once rouse Hor's suspicions, it won't be over easy to manage him. Court told me just now that he almost let on to Hor about old Thacher. That he just began to tell him about Fort Dunbar's being upon his grounds, and your plan of putting the flag there, and how mad the old man would be, because he is suspected of favoring the South, when he remembered in time, and turned off the talk."

"Court's a fool," said Van, impatiently; "but I've got Horace one way if not another. I can show a map so like his that *he* can't tell the difference,—the same paper and all; and then if he does finish his own, and do it well, it 'll be very easy to put in a few last strokes that 'll spoil it all."

"But his private mark?"

"I know what that is: 'Fortune favors the brave;'" and Van drew from his pocket a paper upon which was drawn many times over a miniature shield, inscribed with the motto, "Totis viribus," in tiny letters. Underneath was written H. G., *his mark*. The latter, of course, was not designed to be upon the finished map.

"Now, wasn't it good **luck for** him to drop that one day, just before dress parade, and for me to pick it up 'unknownst' to Hor, and then when **he** asked **me** if I 'd seen it, was n't I *so* anxious to **help him** find it. I asked him if it was very important **to** him, the paper, **you know**, and he said no : **yes, in** one sense **it was ;** it **was his** private **mark** for his map, and he had made **a good** one after much labor, and he wanted it for a copy. I told him I thought it likely **if he lost** it when **we** were on dress parade, it had blown into the river, **as** the wind was in that direction. He seemed quite relieved at that idea, as he **said** he did n't want to get up another, and he wanted to feel sure no one would take that from him. He thought **he** had made **it over so** many **times that** he could easily draw another **like it** without a copy ; that the conceit pleased him, and he **was just** going to tell me what it was when I virtuously stopped him.

"I forget," said he ; "but I should n't be afraid

to trust you." "I dare say not," I replied; "but I don't want you to tell me. Don't you see that it might be a very unpleasant thing for me to know anything about it?"

"He thanked me for my thoughtfulness; and as I was passing his desk the other day, I saw him at work on the same device."

"'With all his might' won't save him from me."

"But I don't see how you can get possession of his map if he succeeds in it?"

"Well, I don't know as you need to see," replied Van, petulantly. "I shall, some way; so don't you worry."

I am sorry to give so much space in my story to the plottings of bad boys; but I wish you to see to what mean, wicked devices a vindictive disposition indulged in will lead. Van and Hal were so blinded by their revengeful feelings that they did n't give a thought to the means employed in attaining their ends.

As for Horace, do you, too, think he was a "guy" to be so easily deceived, to be made to believe that boys, who a few weeks ago had vowed revenge upon him, would now be such kind and disinterested friends?

If he had been mean and revengeful in his disposition, he would have suspected the same traits in others; as it was, he judged them by what would have been his own feelings under the same circumstances. After his passion was over, he would have been heartily ashamed of himself, and would have done all in his power to atone for his fault.

Herbert Vane did not call him a guy, because he was not in the habit of expressing himself in such language; but he did fear that Horace was being duped in some way by the boys, and warned him to beware of them, when Horace described to him, in glowing terms, Van and Hal's kindness.

In answer, Horace said, excitedly, " Now I don't think that's kind of you, Herbert, to be so suspicious of these boys. You don't know them; so how can you judge?"

" Very true, Horace, I don't know them except through you, and I judge from what you have told me about them. This sudden change is what I don't understand."

" It isn't a sudden change; it's been coming on by degrees for weeks, and I don't know what you'd have; because a boy's been wrong and ugly once, it don't follow he's always to be so. I'm sure if that's the way you judge people, you better be done with me at once. I 've done heaps of ugly things in my day."

" I dare say, under the influence of temper. I understand that from my own feelings. I hope I'm wrong about these boys; but it will do you no harm to be cautious."

"I can't keep thinking a boy means mischief when he seems so kind and good. What does Van try and help me for, what does he (Hal and Court, too, for that matter) keep reminding me if I am likely to delay and linger when I ought to be studying, what did he show me his map for, that's so much better than mine? Tell me if you can?" asked Horace, triumphantly.

"I can't tell you," replied Herbert. "I hope you are right; perhaps you are."

Nevertheless, he was not convinced; for every proof Horace gave of the boys kindness to him was so much at variance with his preconceived idea of their characters, that he was more and more persuaded that they had some motive of their own for their course.

"Oh," said Herbert, with flushed face and flashing eyes, as he sat thinking the matter over after Horace had gone, "why am I not like others? why am I caged and confined here? I *know* if I could see those boys and hear them talk, I could convince Horace that they mean him no good. Patience, patience; that must be my motto."

The reconnoissance of Brier Hill had two results. A pretty tough, toilsome march for the Highland Zouaves, who thought if that was play marching, real marching must be tough work indeed, and a firmer conviction on the part of Horace than ever before that Van was a "trump."

Van knew just how far it was safe to flatter Horace; and by a judicious use of praise, and a deference to his opinion, he established his power too effectually for Herbert to weaken it. The plan of the siege of Fort Dunbar was again discussed; and it was agreed that it should take place the next week, that there might still be a fortnight left before the close of the term.

"I shall finish my map first, though," said Horace to Van. "I mean to have it all done before the siege. There's no knowing what may happen; and if I meet with any of the casualties of war, I want to have the comfort of knowing my map's all right."

"So I would. I'd make sure of not being lectured another time," replied Van, cordially.

What high spirits Horace was in now! He was doing better at school. The most fastidious critic could find no fault with the execution of his map thus far. He was having jolly good times in camp, and no danger seemed to menace him from any quarter. Was his picket guard kept well posted? We shall see.

CHAPTER XIII.

THORNTON'S ADVENTURE, AND LEE'S ROMANCE.

MARCH, '62. I have had the pleasure of being taken prisoner,— a pleasure not a little enhanced by my escape from durance vile (literally so you will think it) in less than twelve hours after my capture.

Our army, though not of late engaged in active operations, has yet seen a good deal of skirmishing with the enemy. Some of our supply stores are kept in inconveniently convenient location for raids, and that part of our camp has to be well watched, and strong picket guards are constantly posted. It was my luck to be on picket duty in a recent attempt of the enemy to carry off our stores.

To be of any service when on picket duty, you must necessarily be in an exposed situation, and the chances of being shot down unawares by an unseen enemy, is not a pleasant subject for reflection. I must confess to what I suppose is a nervous feeling at such times. From our ignorance of the country and the most available points of attack, the enemy has a decided advantage over us, as they not only attack us from unexpected quarters, but in case of a repulse know the best places to skedaddle to.

Well, as I was about to tell you, one starlight night as I was doing duty on picket, a ball whizzed in most unpleasant nearness to my head, lodging in fact in a tree just above it. In another moment the alarm was given, and falling back to rejoin our company, we found ourselves surrounded by quite a body of the enemy. We fought like tigers, but they far outnumbered us, and before aid could reach us several of our boys, including Holdfast and myself, were taken prisoners, and as many of the supplies were seized as could be carried off. After a few miles the Rebels found us something of an incumbrance, and left us with a strong guard near a rude cabin, with orders to rejoin them in the morning. I was privileged to have a bed on the hard floor of the cabin, while the others threw themselves on the ground outside, making the best of their fate. I was at a loss to know why I was so favored as to be allowed to come into the cabin, and also to have an extra guard over me in the person of a stout negro. The mystery was explained later. I know not why it was, for it was too dark to see the man's face, but I had an intuitive feeling that he was friendly to me, and to attract his attention I began to moan.

He stooped over me and said, "What's the matter, massa?"

"Oh! my arm,— it's wounded; can't you bind it up with my handkerchief?"

"I'se try, Massa; do bes' I can."

While tying up my bleeding arm (it was nothing but a slight flesh wound), he whispered to me, "Yous 'long to Company C, —— New York Regiment?"

"Yes, my friend, I do, and I should be glad to be back with them now."

"Hush, hush! Yous knows one Massa Lee somebody, I done forgot his name, after all Miss Em'ly said?"

"Yes; what of him?"

"Ise got letter for him from young misses. You take him letter safe to Massa Lee, an' I gib you free if I can."

"But how'll you manage it? I fancy the guards outside have no desire to 'gib me free.'"

"In course not. Dey hate Massa Linkem's men. I don't, an' I want to please Miss Em'ly, too. Don' you stir till I gib de word. But when I knocks over one man, and scream out he running away, den you run for de woods. If yous can't get dere, jis you jump into de pigsty back of dis cabin, stoop down feel board, take hold strap, pull up, jump in, shut down, and stay dere till I done come. Un'stan' dat ar'?"

"Yes, I understand. I shall try hard for the woods; the prospect of a leap into a pigsty is n't alluring."

"Better dan de prisons dey put Massa Linkem's men into."

"What you about there, Virgil," said an imperious voice, the owner of which appeared at the same moment at the door of the cabin.

"O dear, massa, I'se playing doctor, dat's all. Dis man's arm done be hurt drefful bad, sure. I'se trying to help him. We's told to lub our enemies."

"Well, love away, if you like, so long as you don't let him escape. He loves you, I dare say, like the rest of his canting race," garnishing his speech with oaths which I will not soil my paper with transcribing.

"De fac' are," said my sable friend, after this interruption was over, "dat ar' my young massa up big house yonder. I's 'spicious he make lub to Miss Em'ly, an' I's more dan 'spicious she lub Massa Lee bes'. Now keep still dere till you hear great noise; then be wide awake, an' clar out double quick."

The next act in this little drama was an astounding one to Holdfast. He had scorned to lie down on the ground, and stood leaning just outside the cabin door, apparently half asleep, really with every sense alert for a chance to escape.

Virgil went to the door of the cabin quietly, administered a heavy blow on Holdfast's shoulder, which knocked him against the nearest guard, who fell over, then screamed at the top of his voice, "Dere's a pris'ner 'scaping!" and in various ways added so much to the tumult and confusion, that Holdfast improved his opportunity, and took his long legs out of sight shortly. I ran for the woods, as directed; but my pursuers were too quick for me, and I was obliged to avail myself of Virgil's hiding-place. I turned, and passing behind the log cabin leaped into the pigsty, much to the terror of the inhabitants thereof, pulled at the bobbin as directed, and the latch flew up, tumbled in and over on to a bed of corn-husks, and lay there convulsed with laughter at this new phase of military life and at the incongruous thoughts that came rushing to my mind. Wouldn't my mother, gentle and loving as she is, turn up her pretty nose at my redolent garments? What words of love and truth were in the dainty missive safe under the breast of my mire-stained jacket? What did my porcine neighbors think, and what was their language, as they still grunted out their disapproval of my unceremonious disturbance of their swinish slumbers? How I laughed inwardly, too, you may be sure, to think of the discomfited Rebs, who were seeking me in the woods back of the cabin when I wasn't 'thar.'"

"All was quiet" about the cabin at last, and long I lay in masterly inactivity. By-and-by back came some of my pursuers, and among them Colonel Darrell, pointed out by Virgil as "Miss Em'ly's" suitor, who gave strict orders to Virgil to keep close watch after me, as I might be still lurking about.

"The —— Yankee had on the uniform of a private, but he was an officer in disguise. I'll swear

the contemptible Northern mudsills don't raise such privates as he. I'm sure of that," were his parting words to Virgil.

I report this, Horace, for mother's motherly pride.

Virgil answered his master's cautions with an emphatic " Never you fear, massa; be sure I keep one good watch after he. My, how he run into de woods! guess dat ar' what you call out of de frying-pan into de fire, for I's confiding I fin' him yet."

A full half hour passed after the last sound of the Colonel's voice had died away before Virgil opened any communication with me, although he frequently passed back and forth in the rear of the cabin, singing, —

"Carry me back to Ole Virginny."

At last he took a long pole and struck vigorously against my hiding-place, from which I needed no second bidding to escape.

"You done come hurry out quick, massa. Dere's a horse in de woods, an' I show you a bridle-path. You got him safe?"

Him plainly referring to the letter, I answered, "All right, friend;" adding, with a laugh, as I glanced at my mired and odorous garments, "You choose strange entrances to your hiding-places."

"Yes, massa; dat ar' 'bout de only place Massa George (Massa George was the Rebel Colonel referred to above) don care for to poke he long nose into. An' arter all, yous had one narrow escape dis time. When you jumped into de pigsty, and dey squealed so, some ob de men arter you looked in dere an' said 't was mighty queer what they was gruntin' 'bout; an' one of 'em poked bout a while, till I offered to jump in an' see if anybody was dere; an' then he said I was an old black fool to t'ink he could n't tell whether 't was a man or pigs that was dere. Lucky for you, nobody but I an' Scip knows bout dat ar'."

Grasping the hand of my sable friend with the classical name, I said, "Thank you most heartily for your aid, Virgil, whatever your motive."

"Oh, I help ebery one Massa Linkem's men if dey like you, such fine-mannered, fine-spoken gentlemens. (There's another plum for you, mother dear.) But you see, massa, I's hab to make b'leve very much hate yous all, else I could n't help Miss Em'ly; don' you see?"

Virgil led me to the wood, pointed out to me the bridle-path, and observing, I suppose, my quizzical look at the sorry nag, he said, "Him got plenty go in him, massa; jes' you see."

It was as he said, and I soon found myself in my own quarters again, much to the astonishment of my friends, who thought I was already far on the way to a Rebel prison.

I sought Lee out at once, and though my heart

was moved at the pleasure I was about to give him, I still could not refrain from a hearty laugh as I drew out the dainty billet-doux from underneath its outer mire-stained envelope.

Lee fired up at once, and went red in the face as a turkey-cock, and as he caught sight of the familiar hand, said fiercely, "What are you laughing at?"

"Forgive me, Lee," I said. "You'll laugh too when you hear my story. Now read your note, which is, I hope, the bearer of good tidings to you."

"Yes, yes; it can, it must be done. I can get leave of absence, I know; and you'll help me, Thorn, I know you will. You know the way, too, and where to find Virgil," was his hurried address after reading his note.

"Yes," I said, laughing again, "I'll help you, whatever the job is."

"I forgot," said Lee, "that you don't know as much as I do about this affair. Come out and sit on that old stump, and I'll tell you the story. Emily Ray was my early playmate and friend. I do not remember the time when we did not love each other, first with a tender sort of brother and sister affection, which, as we grew older, deepened into a strong, ardent love. The year before this Rebellion broke out, Emily went to Virginia, to teach in the family of a distant relative. When the troubles commenced, she was anxious to return North. She, too, like myself, is motherless; but her relatives persisted in detaining her, and of late she has been kept almost a prisoner. Colonel Darrell, son of Mrs. Darrell, with whom she is, is determined to marry her. *I* unite with her in the determination that he shall not, and his success is consequently more than doubtful. I knew the Darrells lived somewhere in this neighborhood, but I thought it was farther South. Virgil will help us, and, indeed, all the slaves, for Emily has made friends of them. To-morrow night Darrell will be with his regiment. There's no one else to fear, as all the men of the family are absent in the army. There are visitors now at headquarters, who will see Emily safe home when they return to the North, which will be in a day or two. I will get leave of absence for us both, if you will go with me."

"Right gladly will I go with you, Lee, — the sooner the better."

I entertained my companions that evening with my experience while a prisoner, much to their mirth. Holdfast inquired in his usual deliberate manner why in thunder and lightning they could n't have made an opening into the trap, as he called it, in a more decent place.

Pat fired up at this. "An' what should ye be afther wanting a dacenter place than alongst of the pigs, the dear crathurs. Sure an' it's meself has found them better company nor some of yer black gintry there's such hoorahs about."

"*Chacun à son goût*," I ventured to say, in a low tone; and Holdfast shouted out —

"Waal, this is the first time *I* ever heerd of anybody's taking a notion to pigs' company. To my mind pigs is pigs, and that's same's to say the nastiest creturs livin'."

"But that's neither here nor there," said I, laughing, anxious to avert Pat's wrath. "The 'reason why,' was given me by Virgil, — because it was the only place Colonel Darrell would n't ' be poking his long nose into.' If made from the floor of the cabin, or from the outside beyond the pigsty, of course the opening would be discovered."

"Waal, that sounds sensible. A reason's a reason, and satisfies me a heap better than a tarnation string of words with nothing but jabber in 'em," said Holdfast, looking slyly at Pat as he spoke.

Lee easily obtained leave of absence for us both, and on the night appointed we set forth gayly to meet Virgil at the appointed place of rendezvous, the afore-mentioned cabin. He was there, and making a motion of caution, said, —

"De debil and all's to pay. My massa, de Colonel, done come home to-night, an' dere's no cheating him."

"We shall see," said Lee, contemptuously. "Did he bring any of his company with him."

"Neber a one 'cept Jake; and Jake'd like no

better fun dan to see his massa shot down. Jake jes' hates him."

Lee then briefly detailed a new plan of campaign to me, which meeting my cordial approbation, he took Virgil aside and gave him his directions.

"My golly, Massa Lee, neber you fear us; we's all for you an' Miss Em'ly. Jes' take care ob de Colonel, an' we manage de res'. My, dat ar'll be good joke, s'pose you carry him t'rough."

"There's no suppose about it," replied Lee, loftily, "if you negroes do your part. Plenty of noise and confusion, and information the wrong way; do you understand?"

"Yes, massa, I un'stan' dat ar'; an' I un'stan', too, I's to hab de hoss and traps ready in de wood jes' back ob de house. Now you un'stan' you's to go to de right ob de summer-house, not to de lef'?"

"Yes. Be off with you. We'll come in half an hour; they'll be at supper then."

At the expiration of the appointed time we followed Virgil to the old house which gleamed out through the trees about a quarter of a mile distant. There was just light enough from an increasing moon to show us our way without difficulty, and not enough to make us conspicuous to any one who might be on the lookout from the mansion. We went first to the front door, which opened on to the wide piazza, and found that it was as Virgil had promised it should be, slightly ajar; then we crept cautiously round to the back of the house, and looked in through the uncurtained windows at the party at the table. There sat Mrs. Darrell and her daughters, and Colonel Darrell, and beside him Emily Ray. I knew it was she from the pale face and anxious look, and from the quick, short breaths Lee drew.

"The scoundrel!" he muttered, between his set teeth. "Now's your time," he whispered to me. "Make a rush, and if he tries to escape, a bullet'll soon settle him. It's hard to give this up to you," added Lee, jealously.

"O, well," I whispered, "I'd quite as lief take charge of the young lady; it's only to change parts, and let the play go on all the same."

"Don't be a fool!" said Lee, between his set teeth. "Now for it!"

I stepped lightly forward, threw up the long window in an instant, rushed in, walked up to the Colonel, and demanded his sword.

"By what right, you ——* Yankee?" he cried, rising and confronting me.

"By right of might, sir. Will you go peaceably, or shall I order in my company, which I left out of doors, out of respect to the ladies?"

* Keeping my eye upon him, I stepped a little towards the open window, and said, "Corporal

---

* The reader will perceive that I have taken the liberty of borrowing, in part, the recent gallant exploit of a brave Boston boy, and have, of course, made an anachronism.

Trim, to the front of the house, and guard the avenue. Sergeant Cripps, send off five more men to the rear, and remain where you are with the rest. If there's trouble here, come in at once.

Brief as the time was in which this passed, it sufficed for the servants to get up a perfect pandemonium in noise. Cries of " Oh, oh, massa, we's be all murdered! Dere's heaps an' heaps of 'em out dere!" " Oh, missus, what shall we do? Here's Massa Linkem's whole army jes' ober de bridge!" " Oh, my good Lord, dere's Miss Em'ly done gone faint away! Here, you, Lize and Dinah, take her away!" " Oh, dear Lord, is dis de judgmen', comin wid de fire and sword?" And sundry like exclamations, while the women and children shrieked, the dogs barked, and over all rose Colonel Darrell's stern voice,—

" Silence, idiots! To your huts and kennels, and cease this —— din!"

Supposing the house to be actually surrounded, he haughtily begged a moment's talk with his mother.

" It must be but a moment, then," I said, " my time is precious." A few brief words in which I could distinguish some words about Emily's being closely watched, and the haughty scion of one of Virginia's first families, fell into the trap laid for him, and was soon preceding me down the avenue towards the wood. Of course I followed with rifle at full cock ready for any emergency, but devoutly praying such emergency might not arise; for I felt it would be a far different thing shooting a man down in cold blood as it were, to firing on the battle-field, yourself attacked as well as attacking. We had not proceeded far upon our solitary march before he turned partly round and said to me, " where is your company?"

"Here Sir, at your service," I replied. "I am corporal, sergeant, and company. Thornton Grey, private in company C, —— New York regiment." I don't register oaths in these pages, Horace, and I hope your knowledge of wicked words has never gone so far as to enable you to conceive the horrid imprecations that burst from Darrell's lips when he comprehended the trick that had been played upon him; and as yet he knew not that he was foiled in love, as well as in war!

My blood ran cold at his words, and I almost feared his very wickedness would prove more than a match for my arms and watchfulness. It was an anxious march, and I must confess to great relief, when I was met half way to camp, by a strong guard, who took possession of my prisoner, and left me free to breathe and think once more naturally.

Lee, aided by Virgil, had escaped with Emily without much difficulty, though one or two of the slaves who were not in the secret, owing to some uncertainty as to their trustworthiness, made some vigorous resistance at first to her being carried off. Chloe, however, Virgil's mother, and a person of consequence in the colored establishment of Madam Darrell, interfered in time to prevent any serious delay in the lovers' escape. When we reached our tent, Lee and Emily had already gone to headquarters, and the very next day she set out on her journey home under kind and safe escort.

As for Darrell, he was almost beside himself with rage when he learned that Emily had escaped his mother's guardianship. He insisted vehemently upon being allowed to confront Lee; and I was told by Ned, — I beg his pardon, Captain Howe, — who was present, that Lee, although every whit as enraged as Darrell, bore himself far more like a man than the latter. It was a bitter pill for a haughty Rebel to swallow, — to be outwitted in war and love by a couple of Yankee mudsills; for he seemed to forget after this affair the impression my appearance had made upon him previously.

For the rest, I must tell you, because I know that it will gratify you, that I gained a good deal of credit in my regiment for my share in the capture of Colonel Darrell. Our Colonel said — and his praise is not so freely given as to make it valueless — that it was a brave thing for one who was not only in military parlance, but in actual fact, a boy, to do, when my captive was a bold, fearless man, every inch an experienced soldier.

Boy I was when I left home, but boy I am no

longer. Experiences such as ours puts the man into the heart, if there's ever to be a man's spirit in one. I have thus far given you only the froth of my daily life, with here and there a glimpse of something more solid; but you will yet find, I trust, that under all our jollity beat stout, strong hearts.

CHAPTER XIV.

HORACE IS TAKEN PRISONER.

HORACE was in a very critical situation just at this time. Not only was he exposed to the machinations of enemies without, but the very security that he felt that he was now safely guarded from foes within increased his danger. There is a text which every human being should ponder well in their hearts, as a safeguard against temptation, — "Let him that thinketh he standeth take heed lest he fall."

Horace thought his footing was secure. Since the public reproof Mr. Marsh had given him, his lessons, if not thoroughly learned, were at least quite up to the average mark of other boys. Thanks to Herbert's persevering warnings, his mother's gentle reminders, and St. John's interested inquiries respecting his progress, his map was in a very commendable state of forwardness as the time appointed for the siege of Fort Dunbar drew near.

The whole map was neatly outlined, — the loyal States with a faint black line, enclosing a triple row of the loyal colors; while the seceded States were heavily outlined with black only, and beside their gay sisters looked like mourners. Locations already famous for battles were marked by stars, large and full if victories, and small and jagged if they indicated defeat or doubtful success. In one corner was the shield upon which was the motto already described, and which Horace had exultingly pronounced to be done tip-top style, if it was his own work. Just below the motto, written in such tiny letters that no one could distinguish them from a slight ink line unless told what they were, were the initials H. G. In fact, nothing remained to be done but to write out neatly the names of the principal towns, and mark the localities of camps and hospitals, the former to be designated by a tiny row of tents, the latter by a miniature tree.

As Horace looked with gratified pride at his map when it was in the state described, he could not help exultantly saying to Herbert, " Well, you see, old croaker, I'm likely to succeed, after all. Van says there's no fear for me; I shall always pull through whatever I undertake."

" Perhaps you will, only there are different ways of pulling through," said Herbert. " Perhaps my croaking has n't done you any harm."

" Don't say it has; in fact, I dare say I should n't have done so much but for you; but then I could do double the work I have to do on it before the time's up. One would think you were calculating upon my breaking my right arm at least in the siege."

"One can never calculate what may happen," said Herbert, gravely. "I think you are undertaking a perilous feat and a dangerous one, from your own account of the place."

"Of course you think so," retorted Horace, hastily, and in a tone that conveyed more than the words.

Herbert flushed scarlet, and said, quickly, "I know a poor, deformed boy like me is no judge of the sports of active, healthy ones."

"O Herbert, I did n't mean that; at least, I did n't mean to hurt your feelings; I did n't think."

"Never mind; you are very thoughtful generally, Horace, and it was foolish in me to care for what you said then."

This conversation was two days before the long-talked-of siege of Fort Dunbar.

Van, who was determined Horace should not finish his map previous to that event, exerted every means possible to detain him from his work these two afternoons, and he was successful. "After all," said Horace to Herbert, "it is folly to be so set about it. I don't expect to lose my right arm or break my neck in this feat of war; but I'll tell you what, there's so little to be done, I will take it to school, and finish it this morning. I shall have lots of time. I can write better there than anywhere else."

"O, I would n't take it to school, Horace; don't."

"Why not? what can happen to it?"

"I don't know; you may forget it, and leave it there."

"It'll be safe enough if I should. Good by; I'll come in to-morrow, and tell you all about the siege, and show you the map too."

Herbert saw him go with many misgivings, although he could not have told what he feared.

Before recess Van, passing by Horace's desk, saw him with his map spread out before him, and laid his plans accordingly.

The moment school was over, he hurried up to Horace, told him to come with him quickly, for he had something of importance to say. His eager and authoritative manner put everything out of Horace's mind, and books, map, and everything were left to follow Van, and receive some unimportant directions about the ladder to be used in their scaling feat that afternoon.

"All right," said Horace, "but you could have told me this just as well another time. I want to go back now to my desk, and get my books."

Van swore roundly he was a fool to be worrying about his books. "Have a good time for once in your life, can't you? Come along with me."

Horace looked disturbed.

"Well, I shouldn't have sworn if you hadn't kept me waiting. Fact is, if a boy hears swearing at home, he's pretty likely to rip out once in a while himself. You've done me good in that way as well as others," said Van.

This mollified Horace completely, and his companion managed to keep him interested till there was barely time to run home and get the early dinner the boys were to have previous to going to camp.

"I've carried my point, though I don't know what special good it's to do me, for, if I could get the map, it would be no use to deface or change it now; but fortune'll favor me yet, maybe something'll turn up," said Van to himself, as he hurried home.

As for Horace, it was hours before he thought of his map again, and then it was with a bitter pang that he had not followed Herbert's advice.

The boys met at their camping-ground, a beautiful grove in the neighborhood, at the appointed hour, and proceeded to carry out their plan for the siege. They were in the highest spirits, and it was some time before they could get sober enough to observe military decorum. At last the drum beat, the roll was called, they were mustered into rank, and the order was given to shoulder arms and march single file to the river side, to take boats to Fort Dunbar, about half a mile above; for the expedition was to be in part a naval one.

The advance boat was under the charge of Horace, manned by Court and five other boys, who had been detailed for the special duty of scaling and storming the fort, while the remainder of the company were to make a demonstration lower down for the purpose of drawing off the enemy's attention. The enemy was not altogether an imaginary one, as they found after a while to their cost; and even now they were assailed by showers of small stones, dirt, and sand, propelled downwards by certain small boys engaged for the purpose, who were hidden behind protecting shrubs and trees on the sloping side of the precipice. Of course the Highland Zouaves received this formidable repulse with great bravery and abundant demonstration of a noisy nature.

As soon as the boat in which Horace and his companions were touched the shore, he leaped out, and with the aid of the other boys took the ladder out from the bushes where it had been secreted, and placed it in proper position against the wall of rock which rose up before them. Both Van and Horace thought the ladder was quite long enough to reach up to the portion of the rock which, shelving back, would afford a comparatively safe footing. But when Horace reached the last round, he found to his dismay that too long a space still intervened to make it safe to try and reach that part of the precipice. He looked about him in disappointment for a moment, and then saw a place in the rock just above him almost large enough to hold his foot, while still farther up was a thick stunted shrub, of which he was sure he could lay hold if once as high up as the little cleft above mentioned. He coolly took out his knife, opened it, and found that he could easily enlarge the hole sufficiently for his purpose. He did so, left the ladder, placed his foot in the cleft, laid hold of the shrub, which proved a sure support, and was soon on the top of the rock, waving his hat to his excited companions below. It was a perilous feat, and but for his great daring, added to a cool head and steady nerves, it would have been a fatal one. Even Van had trembled with horror when he found the predicament Horace was in, because he knew he would run every risk rather than come down the ladder foiled in his purpose. He did not wish to be the means of his death; he only wished to disgrace him. - It had been no lack of personal courage, or fear of getting into a scrape, that had kept him from taking the post of peril he had assigned to Horace. No, he had been actuated by a far different motive.

Court had wavered in his design to follow Horace, till the acclamations with which his feat was received, and the promptings of a reckless and bold spirit, determined him to follow; and, before Van could interfere, he was already up the ladder, had taken the dangerous leap, was safe beside Horace, and was in his turn greeted with loud applause. The other boys declined following, and no one attempted to induce them to do so.

Captain Van and his soldiers had been so intent upon watching Horace that their part of the play was left unperformed, much to the disgust of the afore-mentioned small boys, who were to personate the enemy. One of them, in particular, — a boy with a fiery red head, and a revengeful face, — muttered to himself, "I've lost the chance this time. My little stone would have been a big un for him. You'll cotch it yet, Cap'n Van, and larn not to meddle with me."

The next proceeding on the part of the successful assailants was to let down a cord, by means of which the flag was to be drawn up. This was done, and the two boys soon had it flying from the topmost branch of a tree which stood on the very summit of the rock. Three cheers and a tiger were next proposed by the company below for the brave besiegers of Fort Dunbar, and then they all made the shores and rocks resound with America.

It was now sunset, and Horace was just consulting Court as to the best way of getting down, by a path with which Court had said he was familiar, when he was startled by his companion's exclaiming, "Come away, Horace, quick, or you'll be killed!" and at the same instant came a flash, and a loud report, and Horace fell to the ground, blinded and stunned.

The next act in this performance, which seemed to be fast turning into a tragedy, was equally astounding to both boys.

A rough-looking man, accompanied by two huge dogs, appeared from the wood beyond, and, roughly shaking Court, asked him how he dared to be trespassing on private property, raising flags and the devil at the same time.

Court answered, angrily, that he was n't trespassing, and that there had been no harm done, — the boy was only stunned.

The man swore he did n't care what became of the boy, but they were to go with him. Horace, who was now somewhat recovered from the shock of the explosion, and the effects of a blow on the temple from a piece of stone, rose to his feet, and attempted to explain.

"Ye need n't waste yer words on me. The notice 's up plain as day, the farther end of these woods, that there 's no trespassing allowed. Ef 't aint trespassing to yell like devils, string up —— flags, and blow up rocks, without leave, I should like to know what is."

"I did n't know," said Horace, Fort Dunbar was in Mr. Thacher's woods; and I don't know any more than yourself about the rock's blowing up."

"A likely story! Come along. No; I guess, though, as you've taken a fancy to call this here rock a fort, I 'll see ef I can't find a dungeon for you. Pity to spile good sport!"

"But I'm hurt, and burned, too," pleaded Horace. "Don't leave us here to-night."

"One of the fortins of war, I guess," said the man, with a savage grin. "Ye'll have to try and see how you like it."

In vain Horace begged him to have compassion on his state; equally in vain did Court swear and threaten the man with his father's vengeance. He made no answer, but coolly dragged Horace along to the edge of the wood, motioning Court to follow, and, opening the door of a small building, roughly put the boys in, and calling one of the dogs to him, said, "Lie down there, sir, till I come to you!" pointing to a spot just outside the door. Then, turning to the boys, with the words, "Ef ye try to git away, he'll tear you to pieces," left them to their fate.

CHAPTER XV.

BITTER FRUITS.

For a moment neither of the boys spoke, and then Horace asked, angrily, of Court —

"What does all this mean? Are we on Mr. Thacher's grounds, and what was the cause of the explosion? You know we were forbidden the use of powder when we first got up our company."

"Only in firearms," replied Court.

"You know that is a pitiful equivocation; it was not intended we should use it at all. You will oblige me by telling me how this happened. I cannot take it quite as coolly as you do, seeing that I am badly burned."

"Well," said Court, sulkily, "Van said it would be nice fun to have a salute fired just as the flag was raised; and so he had a little powder placed in a crevice in a rock, and after you had climbed the tree, I was to apply a slow match to it. Van calculated it would go off about the time we were ready to come down; but it went off sooner than we expected, and you were close by the rock before I knew it. I did call out as soon as I could; but it was no use, — it was too late. As for old Thacher, I knew these were his woods, but I did n't suppose he kept guard here. I dare say Van did, though, now I think of it; for he was mighty sly in all his doings up here, would only go at certain hours, and all such things. I wish I knew, guess I 'd tell a thing or two that would make him repent playing his tricks on me."

"Well," said Horace, contemptuously, "Van and Hal have made a cat's paw of you. I begin to 'see it' now. Herbert was right. Oh, what a fool I have been!"

"A cat's paw, indeed! If I thought they had, should n't they repent it! Well, if I 'm a cat's paw, you 've been a fool over and over again. They 've been imposing upon you for weeks, and just trying to do all they could to injure you. Yes, I 'see it' too, now. They wanted me to help them, and did n't care how big a scrape they got me into."

And here Court began to curse and swear and stamp with impotent rage, to which the dog responded with loud and prolonged barking; and Horace, smarting and blinded from the effects of his burn, his limbs aching, and his heart swelling at the treachery practised against him, sternly bade Court be silent and let him think.

Thinking was of little comfort or help to him, however. There was no chance for escape, in his condition; for, even had he dared to encounter the dog, he was too weak and dizzy to do so, with any prospect of success. The more he thought of his present condition, and the schemes that had brought him to it, the more angry and mortified he was. At last anger with his companions gave place to the voice of conscience, and indignation at himself. Appearances were all against him. What would his parents and Herbert say to his declaration that he did n't know Fort Dunbar was on Thacher's grounds. Why did n't he know? Why had he gone blindly into the trap set for him? Of what avail now were all his attempts to regain his character at school. Though he was not guilty of any great wrong, yet the situation he was now in was owing to his careless manner of looking into things, his neglect of wise counsel, his ready ear to the voice of flattery, which had blinded his judgment, and made him a willing dupe of wicked, designing boys. He thought, too, of Thornton, and his advice to keep his pickets well posted, and to beware of insignificant foes. He thought of all these things, and then, as if to fill his cup of bitterness to the very brim, there flashed into his mind the recollection of his map, in his desk at school, unfinished! If he had kept to his original plan of working upon it with diligence till it was completed, this anxiety, at least, would have been spared to him. And Horace groaned again in agony of spirit. The smart from his wounds was less painful than his regrets. There could be no hope now that he could finish his map. He felt sure that his eyes were injured, for a time, at least; and even if Mr. Marsh was willing, on account of his accident, to overlook its unfinished state, what security had he that he should find it safe in his desk as he left it? Why had Van been so anxious to see it? Why had he examined it so closely? What a deep-laid plan Van's was! Who but Herbert, who had warned him against these boys, would believe that they were guilty, and he innocent, when they had been making marked progress in school, while he had been publicly censured for his neglect!

Ah! Horace, Horace, the little faults you have sown so lavishly have become a heavy harvest for you to reap! The little events of your daily life, which you might have controlled to your highest good, resisting temptation, and strengthening your character, you have suffered to control you!

Little things they may seem to you, my young friends, who read this record, and scarcely worth so many words, since you cannot see that Horace did anything very wrong, after all. So they seemed to him, at the time; so they do not seem to him now in their results. And he thinks, as he sits in darkness and suffering, that he shall never, never again be so easily led away from the straight path of right, or be so easily duped.

And thus the slow hours lag on, and Court's expressions of rage at his companions' meanness are unheeded by Horace, and unnoticed save by the responsive growl of Lion, who at each loud tone of the incensed boy, lets him know that he is alert and vigilant.

Meantime, where are the Highland Zouaves? A brave and reliable company, surely, thus to leave their companions in peril.

When Van and Hal heard the loud report from the explosion of the rock, the barking of the dogs, and the angry voice of the man, they began to fear that their work of mischief was a little overdone, and they held a short consultation as to the next step to be taken. Some of the boys wished to rush up at once, by a side path, to the summit of the rock and rescue their comrades; but Van vetoed this plan. The man or men, and the dogs, would be more than a match for them; they would only get themselves into trouble and not aid their companions. No, the the only thing to be done was to notify Mr. Grey, and Mr. Warrenton, Court's father, of the flight of their sons. This Van undertook to attend to himself, and desired the other boys to go quietly home, and say as little as possible about the affair.

But Van was in no hurry to inform the gentlemen of what had happened,— he hardly knew how to frame his story so as to screen himself from all blame. Consequently it was dark before he reached Mr. Grey's home, which was the most distant one, and told his story. Mr. Grey did not ask many questions or make many comments upon Van's account of the matter, but he regarded him sternly and hastened to Mr. Warrenton's.

Mr. Warrenton did n't take the matter so quietly, but said angrily that they were a pretty set of fellows to put two boys to the most difficult part of their enterprise, and then desert them in the time of difficulty. It seemed that nothing was to be done but go direct to Mr. Thacher. He received them very gruffly, and at first refused to allow the boys to be liberated, appearing to consider their imprisonment, not only as a good joke, as his man had regarded it, but also a well-merited punishment for trespassing.

Mr. Grey replied that the punishment might be a deserved one, but it was running some risk of the boys' lives to leave them all night in such a place; that he would see that his son was punished according to his fault, and that he would pay any fine for trespassing Mr. Thacher thought proper to require.

Upon this Mr. Thacher yielded, saying, in an undertone, it was more than he 'd have done for any other man in the neighborhood, as Mr. Grey was the only one who knew how to mind his own business.

He then had his man called, and the party set off through the woods to the place of the boys' imprisonment.

Mr. Grey was shocked indeed to find Horace lying insensible upon the ground, his face blackened with powder and stained with blood from the cut on his forehead.

Van had merely mentioned the explosion in a careless manner; and, in fact, he did not know that Horace had been burned. Court gave but a lame account of the matter. Mr. Warrenton swore roundly that the whole affair should be looked into, and that those who had made scapegoats of the others should pay dearly for it. Mr. Grey, as before, expressed his indignation only in his countenance, which grew more and more stern.

Horace was taken home as quickly as possible, and upon examination the cut was found to be slight, and the bruises not very serious; but he was chilled and exhausted from his exposure to the night air and the fatigue he had undergone, and before morning was in a high fever, raving of sieges, scaling walls, and explosions.

CHAPTER XVI.

VAN WINS THE PRIZE.

Now, according to the most approved style of story-writing, I should leave Horace in the midst of his troubles and return to Thornton. But I cannot desert him now in his dark hour, and hasten to relate how he came out into light again.

Poor boy! his fever ran high, — little knew or cared he about the tender love and anxious fears that kept watch night and day by his bedside. All things had but one meaning to him; all faces but one expression. He was fighting battles against treacherous foes. The idea of treachery seemed uppermost in his mind, for he was particularly averse to those who regarded him with the most interest; and one day when his mother, with anguish in her heart but a smile on her lips, bent over him to perform some office of love, he motioned her away with every appearance of dislike, and said: "You smile, and I know what that means; it means deception. Yes, a man may smile, and smile, and be a villain."

Then, tossing restlessly upon his bed, he would

call out — " Beware of the rocks, the woods, the fields, there's an enemy there; he is everywhere. O, why do you not drive him away. Don't you see him grinning at me from behind that wall of rock ?' pointing, as he spoke, to a half open door. " Mark, he's filling that tree with powder; don't you hear it go off? Take care, you'll be killed just as I was. I was killed the other day, but I had to come to life to finish my map, and now no one will bring it to me. Why *don't* you bring it to me; O, the enemy's got it, has he ? I thought so."

He raved so much of his map that Mr. Grey sent over to ask Herbert Vere about it. Herbert told of his taking it to school the last day he went. Mr. Grey sent for it, and it was found safe in his desk, neatly rolled and tied with a blue ribbon his mother had given him for that purpose.

Mr. Grey examined the map, and passing it to his wife, said, — " It is well begun and the shield and motto are finely executed, but the names of places are carelessly written, and there are blots and marks upon it. What a pity Horace should have neglected his work for these boys, who, I fear, have been playing a double part."

" Cannot you find out about the matter," asked Mrs. Grey, anxiously.

" No, Court says he knew they were on Thacher's grounds, but he did n't suppose it was any harm, and he did n't think Horace thought it was either. Now,

Horace *knew* it was wrong if he knew whose land he was upon. I have questioned Van and Hal, and can find out nothing against them but the cowardly part they acted in the end of the affair. It seems to me Court knows more than he chooses to tell; as for the other boys in the company, it is plain they have told all they do know. If Horace recovers the matter shall be thoroughly sifted. He will tell the truth, at all events. If he does not, some way will be opened to us to discover all the facts of the case.

"If," repeated Mrs. Grey, with pale face and tearful eyes —

"Yes, Annie," replied Mr. Grey, sadly, "it is, *if.* Horace's situation is very critical, but we will remember that our boy is in the hands of his heavenly Father."

Mr. Grey had not been able thus far to find out the truth of the late disastrous affair to Horace. For Court, who had been so angry with the other boys on the night of his imprisonment, had been very easily intimidated by them into keeping their counsel, and, as they declared, his own as well. "For," said Van, "you have gone into this thing with us from the first; you knew all about it that we knew, for of course we neither expected nor wished the matter to end as it did. All we wanted was to put Horace foremost in the affair so that old Thacher would vent his rage upon him, and thus get the sneak into disgrace with his particular, proper old Dad."

This was true, and Court, who was really a coward, feared the other boys too much to betray them, and faithfully promised to 'keep dark' whatever was said.

So time passed, and Horace still lay on his sick-bed in a critical state when the day came fixed upon for the examination of the maps. Mr. Marsh sent a note to Mr. Grey, requesting him to send Horace's map, adding, if it was nearly finished and proved to be better executed than the others, he saw no reason why it should not take the prize under the circumstances.

"There is not a shadow of a chance for Horace," said Mr. Grey, when he read the note.

"Why, then," anxiously asked Mrs. Grey, "do you send it?"

"Because, I think it right to do so," he replied, "as Mr. Marsh has sent for it. Had it been well executed throughout we should gladly have sent it. That part of it is very carelessly done is a misfortune, and a fault, too, but one that we have no right to conceal. If the lesson it can teach is not for Horace it may be for another."

The examination of the maps resulted in Van's being pronounced the best, without a dissenting voice. When this was announced to the school by Mr. Lewis, a friend of Mr. Marsh's, from the city, and a stranger to all the boys, he added, that while giving the prize to the owner of the map marked with two crossed swords, the committee must admit that a part of the execution of the one which bore the motto *Totis viribus* within a shield, was really superior to that of the one which had gained the prize. "So much superior," he continued, "that I regret it should be defaced by such evident marks of haste and carelessness. I am afraid the lad whose work it is lacks perseverance, a grievous feature in any character. Let me advise him in future to take as much pains in finishing as beginning whatever he undertakes."

Alas, he knew not that the boy whose work he was criticising was lying even then between life and death, and that a few more hours would determine whether his right hand would ever hold pen or pencil more.

It was even so, for the crisis of his disease was at hand, and in tearful prayer his parents awaited their heavenly Father's will.

Van received the books with ill-concealed triumph, and walked homeward with Hal, exulting that their schemes had been successful. "If Horace gets well and declares he did n't leave his map in such a state, it 'll be no use — there 's nothing to prove his words, and all his careless habits are against him," said Van.

"Yes," said Hal, "and if he does n't the matter 's done with; we 've carried this through and I 've had enough of it for one, and mean to let him alone in future. I hope he won't die; it gives me an ugly feeling to think of that; it was a mean thing, as Court says, to leave them there by themselves."

"Oh, get out with your scruples, the day after the fair," said Van, angrily. "You were ready enough then to leave them; and as we did n't know they would be kept there in the damp so long, how are we to blame, I should like to know?"

"At least, you might have let his map alone," said Hal. "That was mean when he was sick in his bed; I'm sorry I helped you, there."

"Shut up with you; how do you know who's passing us. I thought he'd be out in a day or two when I did it, and I wanted to fix him out both ways, — what's done's done, and it's no use to repent of it."

"No," said Hal, with a sneer, "certainly not, when one has gained a handsome set of books by it."

CHAPTER XVII.

TRUTH PREVAILS.

But I leave these boys to their quarrel, which waxed hotter and hotter till they parted, mutually enraged with each other, and return to Mr. Marsh, who, when he was alone in his schoolroom, took up Horace's map and regarded it with a stern yet sorrowing face.

"Too bad, too bad, and the boy was so capable," said he unconsciously aloud. At this moment he heard a slight noise, and raising his eyes saw at the door two boys, the smaller of whom came forward, while the larger remained at the door.

"What do you want?" asked Mr. Marsh.

"Want to tell you suthin," was the gruff answer.

"What is it? speak, for I am in haste," said Mr. Marsh quickly, for the boy's appearance, coarse, ragged, and dirty as he was, was not prepossessing.

"I knows all about that 'ere map, the sick un's, I mean."

"You, how?" was the astonished reply, "and who are you?"

"My name's Josh Grew."

Now, Josh Grew was the small boy who, upon the day of the attack of Fort Dunbar, had been heard to utter threats against Van, but of this Mr. Marsh knew nothing. Out of a spirit of wanton mischief, not because he cared which of the two was right, Van had one day interfered between this boy and a larger one in a quarrel, taking the part of the larger. Josh neither forgot nor forgave this act, and even as Van had done with Horace, so had his smaller foe watched for his opportunity of revenge.

From time to time he had heard scraps of talk between Van and Hal, and sometimes Court, that soon put his keen wits upon a track that he thought would lead to revenge. But he knew full well that his own character for truth was by no means so good among those who knew him as to have his word taken against boys so far removed from him in social position, as well as in reputation. While casting about in his prematurely cunning brain how he should remedy this defect in his evidence against Van, accident threw an opportunity in his way, of which he was not slow to avail himself.

The conversation which ensued between Mr. Marsh and the two boys will be inferred from what follows.

The next day everything passed off as usual in school till twelve o'clock, when Mr. Marsh requested the boys to lay aside their books, as he had something of importance to communicate to them.

When this order was obeyed with wondering

astonishment by the pupils, Mr. Marsh stood up on his desk and looked around upon the scholars with an air of deep feeling, and addressed them as follows: —

"Boys, the matter to which I wish to call your attention is one of great importance to me, and I hope it will prove to be no less so to you, since it involves the character of one of your schoolmates now lying dangerously ill. I do not doubt many of you think that the faults of which Horace Grey has been deemed guilty are trifling in their nature. In fact, so much so, as to make it unadvisable to refer to them. You, none of you, think it a very bad thing to trespass upon the grounds of a neighbor whom you think unsocial or disobliging. You, none of you, think carelessness in habits, or neglect of lessons, a very grave fault.

"Yet it is certain, if Horace Grey *knowingly* trespassed upon Mr. Thacher's grounds, he committed the double fault of disobedience to his father's commands and infringing upon the rights of another.

"These misdemeanors, even your boyish habits of viewing leniently *small* faults, as you call them, cannot excuse. As for carelessness and neglect of study, I consider them grave errors in themselves, and the evils to which they lead are legion, and their results lifelong.

"But my present object is to lay before you a few facts, which in a most unexpected manner have come to my knowledge, and then I shall leave you to decide whether Horace is guilty of the charges that have been brought against him."

A breathless silence pervaded the schoolroom at these words. Eager looks were interchanged, and Van, who had at first glanced triumphantly at Hal, as much as to say, "he's got to be publicly disgraced now," changed countenance, and looked alarmed and anxious.

Mr. Marsh continued: "Van Dusen Whitmore, Courtland Warrenton, and Harry Gierson, you are accused of being engaged in a conspiracy against Horace Grey's character; of endeavoring to seduce him from his duties; of making him, unknown to himself, commit an unwarrantable trespass upon a neighbor's grounds; and finally, of defacing the map which he had partially completed, thus causing him to appear guilty of great carelessness.

"The first witness I shall summon against you is Stephen Harwood. You best know whether his evidence will be in your favor or against you. Stephen Harwood, have you any reason to suppose that there has been a conspiracy among these boys against Horace Grey?"

Stephen rose in his seat, no less astonished at being called upon, than the guilty boys were that he should be, and said: "Some weeks ago, sir, I knew there was something of the sort growing out of the foolish scrape to which I also was a party. But I have heard nothing of it of late, or seen any indications that they bore Horace any ill-will. On the contrary ——"

"That is sufficient on that point. Confine yourself in your evidence strictly to answering the questions that are asked. Relate the circumstances of that affair to which you allude as accurately as possible."

Stephen gave the account with which my readers are already familiar, taking care this time not to add any of his own impressions.

When he had finished, Mr. Marsh said: "Now, I wish to ask you what knowledge you have of their feelings towards Horace of late, or rather, what your impressions upon that point are?"

"I have noticed proofs of marked friendliness, sir, towards Horace."

"What effect did this altered course of conduct have upon your mind?"

"It surprised me at first, because it was so unexpected; but after a while I supposed they had forgotten the affair, and in consequence I ceased to feel any more anxiety about Horace."

"Why was it unexpected? boys often quarrel furiously and then are good friends immediately afterwards."

"If you will excuse me, sir, I should prefer not to answer that question, except by saying it arose from my knowledge of the parties concerned."

A half smile stole over Mr. Marsh's face, as if the answer was quite sufficient for him, but it was instantly repressed, and he said, "That will do Stephen, — you may sit down."

Mr. Marsh then rang a bell, and the door opened and three boys entered. Slouching, spiteful, and leering sideways at Van, came Josh Grew, followed by Joe Lane, a poor boy, well known to Mr. Marsh for his steady, industrious habits, and Tom Dale, who took charge of the schoolroom.

"Come forward, Joshua Grew, and tell me what you know of a plot against Horace Grey," said Mr. Marsh.

"I knows I've heerd them boys talk it over in the woods and down by the shore, lots of times. They said as how they'd fix out Horace Grey yet; that they never forgot a grudge; that he should pay yet for spiling their fun. I heerd em say as how they'd make him go up to old Thacher's woods, and put a flag on the tallest tree there; that the old man was a southern suthin — I forget what — only I made out he'd be all-fired mad to see the Union flag a waving on his trees. They said he was such a careless, reckless dog, he'd never know whether he was on Queen Victory's grounds or whose; that his father'd be tarnation mad with him, as well as Skinflint, and old Marsh. I heerd 'em say, too, they'd spile his map for him if he did n't spile it hisself. Leastways, they all talked about these 'ere things,—

but that one, pointing **to Van**, seemed to be most spiteful like."

"How came you to hear all this; you must have been **spying**?" asked **Mr. Marsh**, when the boy had got to the end of his volubly delivered story.

"I was in the woods one day when two on 'em, Van and Hal, came along and I heerd suthin about it then, so I tracked 'em urterwards and used to hide and listen."

"What was your object in pursuing such a mean course?"

"O, **curosity, I** 'spect, to begin with; and then I **owed** Van a grudge and thought **this** 'ud pay it off."

"How then do you expect your story to be believed, if you own that you **owe a boy** a grudge?" asked Mr. Marsh, severely.

"Did n't never 'spect nobody **to** 'bléve me, **as** nobody never does; but I thought I'd kinder frighten 'em about it arter I'd heerd all I wanted to. But as good luck 'd have it, a boy came along one day folks' could 'bleve, and as soon as **I** see him, says I, 'bully for you, Joe Lane, you's the chap.' But he was goin' on straight ahead, **and** says I ' no you don't;' says he, ' yes I am, I'm **in a** hurry.' ' O, says I, very well; then you don't want to help git Horace Grey out of a big scrape, do you?' 'What?' says he, stopping short. 'That's so,' says **I**, '**an**' then I telled him all I knew, an' what **I** wanted him for, an' that I knowed the boys 'd be 'long soon. He can tell the rest hisself."

Mr. Marsh then requested Joe to tell all he knew about the affair in question.

Joe rose with evident unwillingness and said, "It's just as Josh tells you, sir. I was plaguey loth to turn listener, for it ain't in my line; but I'd do anything to serve Horace Grey, for he's been real kind to me, and his mother'd helped my mother when she was in a deal of trouble. So, when the boys came down to the shore, as Josh thought they would, I heard Van say to Master Hal, 'It's about all fixed now; he's as ready as can be to run headlong into my trap. When he's performed the gallant exploit I keep cramming him with, of scaling Fort Dunbar, and planting the flag in the enemy's country (poor fool, he don't know it is the enemy's in earnest), I guess he'll have to come down a peg in old Marsh's estimation, as well as his governor's. As to his map — we shall see.'"

"How came you to hear so distinctly?" asked Mr. Marsh. "It seems very careless in boys who have a plot against another to talk so freely of it out of doors."

"Why, sir, they did speak low, and could see all around them, but we were perched behind a rock over their heads. It was n't a likely place to be looking out for listeners."

"What more do you know about this matter?"

"Well, sir, the day after the Fort Dunbar scrape Josh came to me and wanted me to go into the woods over there, that side of the schoolroom. He said there was more mischief brewing, and I must go and find it out. So I came and hid behind a tree just over by that window, sir," pointing, as he spoke, to a large tree opposite a window which commanded a view of a row of desks, in the range of which was the one occupied by Horace Grey. "I heard steps, and presently Hal came up and went into the lower schoolroom, and seemed to be looking for something, and then I heard him ask Tom to go up to the recitation rooms and help him hunt for his pencil. I heard them go up stairs; they made a good deal of noise; and then, two minutes after, Van came in and went to a desk over there — I don't know exactly which one — and took out a roll tied with a blue ribbon and put it into his pocket, and then slipped out as fast as he could and came into the wood where Josh and me were hiding. I was scared for fear he'd find us; but luckily he wanted to hide where he could see the schoolroom door. Presently out came Hal whistling, and he joined Van in the woods, and I heard Van say 'all right; come to-morrow morning and I'll bring the map back after I've finished it for Horace,' and then they both laughed. So I came early in the morning, too, with Josh, and got behind the same tree, and pretty soon along came Hal again and waited till Tom came up. Then he said, 'let me in to the schoolroom, will you? I can't find my gold pencil and it *must* be here.' So Tom let him in, and I saw him rummaging about, but I could n't hear what he said because the windows were shut; but pretty soon the two went off up stairs again, though Tom looked as if he did n't like to over-much. Then Van comes in as before, and puts back the roll into the desk, and looks about kind of scared and runs out, and walked off a little way from the schoolroom down by the brook."

"How do you know, as you could not see him pass around the schoolroom?" inquired Mr. Marsh.

"No, sir, I could n't, but I saw him in the path after he got beyond the schoolroom."

"Why should he have gone that way instead of the way he came?"

"To avoid meeting any one, sir."

A peculiar expression passed over Mr. Marsh's countenance at this reply, which no one but Van could interpret,— that he could, was evident from the crimson flush that overspread his face.

"Is this all?"

"Yes, sir, and I hope you'll believe that I never did such a mean thing before as to follow boys about and spy on them, and that I would n't have done it now for anything else than to save Horace from being blamed for what he did n't know was wrong, and for what he did n't do. And I heard, too, he was sick and might die."

"Yes, I believe you, Joe, and so I think do all present," said Mr. Marsh, looking around upon the eager faces upraised to his.

"Now, Tom, what have you to say?"

"I don't know nothin' 'bout it, sir, 'cept what Joe jist telled you 'bout Hal's comin' to look for his pencil. It was jist as he said, and I didn't see Van nor him nother, an' I didn't know they was about. I know I was pretty cross to hev to leave my work an' go an' help him find his pencil; an' now it seems it was jist to cheat me. I calls it real mean, I does."

"That will do, Tom. You can retire boys," said Mr. Marsh, motioning to the three witnesses. I have now a little evidence of my own to give upon this matter, and then we will hear if the accused have anything to say in their defence. In consequence of an interview that I had with Josh and Joe yesterday noon, I took Horace Grey's map over to Mr. Vane's, as I knew that Horace had done a great deal of the work upon it there in Herbert's room. Herbert told me that when Horace took the map from his room, which was the day of the siege of Fort Dunbar, there was not a name written upon it, and that he was very positive that the handwriting, though very similar to his friend's, was not his, in proof of which he showed me several notes that Horace had written to him, and I agreed with him in his opinion.

I know that Horace brought his map to school, for

I noticed at recess that he sat in his desk at work, and I went to him and told him that he must take his recess. I glanced inadvertently at his map as I stood there, and observed that there were no names written upon it then. After recess I gave the boys an unexpected lesson to learn, and Horace had no more time to work upon it. When I looked at the map previous to its examination by the committee, I supposed that he had written the names hastily at noon, and that this accounted for the blots upon it and the careless writing. You now see that such could not have been the case. One word more and my evidence is given. The morning upon which Joe Lane states that the map was returned to the desk by Van, I met him about an eighth of a mile from the schoolroom, in the path leading by the brook. This path Joe Lane also saw him take, as you have heard.

I now call upon the accused to answer for their share in this affair; and first —

"Van Dusen Whitmore, what have you to say in your defence?"

"I say," said Van angrily, rising and facing Mr. Marsh almost defiantly, "that you've got a pretty set of witnesses together, beginning with a thief, liar, and blackguard; for Steve's evidence amounts to nothing, as you well know. A pretty set, indeed, to testify against a gentleman's son! And I say that I've nothing to urge in my defence. My case is prejudged, and I don't expect justice from you."

"And you, Harry Gierson?"

"I say, Sir, that I am heartily ashamed of the part I've taken in this affair, and that if I'd have known the mean things I should do when I began, I wouldn't have had any share in it, — but somehow I was so mad with Horace I only thought of paying him off. And I beg your pardon, Sir, for what I've done, and I will beg Horace Grey's, too, if I ever get the chance."

"Courtland Warrenton?"

"O, please don't punish me, Sir, or send me away from school. I got into the scrape, and Van and Hal kept threatening me all the time if I didn't stay by them. I beg your pardon, and I wont do so another time."

"Boys," said Mr. Marsh, "if any among you think your schoolfellows have been wrongfully accused, you are at liberty to say so."

An ominous silence pervaded the schoolroom.

"Then I proceed to pronounce sentence upon you.

Van Dusen Whitmore, yours is expulsion from the school which you have disgraced, not only because you have been the leader in this conspiracy against an innocent boy, but because you show neither penitence nor a desire to make reparation for your offence.

Harry Gierson and Courtland Warrenton, I accept your apologies, and I will retain you in school upon probation. It rests with yourselves whether or not you remain permanently.

Van Dusen, if at any future time you should wish to return to my school you can do so, by acknowledging your fault in a full confession, and promising future amendment. For your sake I hope Horace Grey will recover. The knowledge that through a persistent determination to injure his character you were indirectly the cause of his death, would be a grievous remembrance for you. Take, I beseech you, this lesson home to your heart —

> "Truth crushed to earth will rise again.
> The eternal years of God are hers."

Here you have gone on, week after week, weaving a tissue of falsehoods, flattering and deceiving a boy of an open and unsuspicious nature, apparently successful in the end you sought to gain, when lo, mysterious power of retribution! a witness rises up against you in the form of a vindictive boy, whom in a moment of wanton tyranny you had injured. As revenge prompted you to plot against a companion whose sole fault was adherence to duty, so the same passion prompts a keen-witted child, schooled in arts and cunning, to plot in his turn against you, and bring your schemes to the light of truth. You have failed in the hour of your greatest triumph. He has succeeded, and the majesty of truth is vindicated. Reflect upon this affair, I beg of you, and do not give yourself up to the dominion of evil passions.

"Boys," continued Mr. Marsh, in a deep, solemn voice, looking around upon his scholars as he spoke, "I do not think you need one word of comment from me upon what you have just heard. You can now lay aside your books and return to your homes. For myself, I shall go to Mr. Grey's at once. I hope to-morrow to bring you good tidings from Horace, — I mean what you will call good tidings, — in any event it will be well with him."

My readers can imagine the confusion and babel of voices that ensued upon the boys finding themselves in the open air, free to give expression to their long pent-up feelings of astonishment, indignation, and satisfaction. The whole matter was so strange to them, — no one but Steve had ever dreamed of any ill-will towards Horace upon the part of the guilty boys. They expressed themselves in the unmeasured terms of condemnation which boys use when once fairly aroused to indignation. Steve was surrounded and questioned; but he said his head ached, he was sick, and he had told already all he knew. Van had taken his books, and walked off with an air of injured pride. Harry lingered till the other boys had left Steve, and then went up to him, and they walked slowly away through the wood, striking out upon the path which led to the brook. As for Court, he sneaked off home by himself, trying not to believe that the words he overheard: "pitiful sneak, coward, cat's paw," &c. were applied to him.

Mr. Marsh went to Mr. Grey's, and in answer to his earnest inquiries about Horace, was told by his father that the crisis was past, and that he was slowly recovering. Mr. Grey's surprise at Mr. Marsh's report of the events of the morning was only equalled by his gratitude that the whole mystery with regard to his son was cleared up.

CHAPTER XVIII.

HORACE MANIFESTS AN UNFAILING SIGN OF CONVALESCENCE.

Horace's recovery was very tedious. The fever had fed upon his fresh, young life, and when it left him he was the shadow of his former self. His mental sufferings, too, were as great as his physical. Those of you who have passed through a violent fit of sickness, know how hard getting well is, — how the limbs ache, how the head throbs and tires at the least thought and exertion, how the grasshopper is a burden; and you scarcely feel grateful for the boon of a life that day after day is such a weariness to you. How irritable you are; how you rebel against the kind and needful restrictions of parents and friends; and you see everybody and everything through the distorted medium of a feeble body and weak nerves. All this Horace felt, and he had other troubles too. As soon as he recovered his senses, after the crisis in his disease was over, he felt a great weight upon his spirits, for which he could not account; for the past was very confused to him, and nothing stood out clearly in his remembrance. But this confusion passed away in a few days, and every event preceding his sickness flashed distinctly into his mind. He was not much troubled at the remembrance of the trespass he had committed upon Mr. Thacher's grounds, although it was, as he acknowledged, owing to his careless way of rushing into things without sufficient forethought; but he knew that he was innocent of any intention to do wrong, and he knew, too, that his father and mother would believe him when he told them so.

But he was very much disturbed when he thought of his map, and the unfinished state in which he had left it; for he had staked much more upon his success in winning the prize for the map than any one knew. He did not, as he told Van, care so very much for the prize in itself, but he did care for it as an honorable testimonial from his teacher, and as a proof to him and his parents that he could overcome his careless and dilatory habits. O, why had he not attended to his first resolution, to finish it entirely before he engaged in anything likely in any way to draw off his attention from it. He could just as easily have finished it before the siege of Fort Dunbar as not, by the practice of a little resolution.

He wished to know the result of the examination, whether after all his map, unfinished though it was, might not have been admitted with the others. And the boys who had schemed against him, all of whose plots and cunning devices were now clear as day to him, had they been found out? Why didn't somebody tell him?

So he grew more and more moody and irritable, answering only in monosyllables his mother's and Margaret's kind inquiries, and efforts to interest and amuse him. At last he could bear this state of suspense no longer, and one day said abruptly to his mother, "Who got the prize for the map — Van?"

"Yes," she answered, surprised at the question, and wondering whether he had been brooding over that, and making himself unhappy when they had carefully avoided any allusion to it, lest it should annoy him.

He made no reply, but his mother, seeing the disturbed expression of his face, added, — Yes, Van got the prize; undeservedly, however, as it proved. You shall hear the whole story when you are strong enough to bear it."

"I am strong enough now. Please tell me; you would if you only knew how the thought of it haunts me day and night."

."Your father will tell you if he thinks it best."

"It is best, — worrying about it just keeps me back; **I want to** know all about it. I thought you'd know I did, and tell me before." This was said in one of his crossest tones, and with the air of a person who feels that he has been injured.

Tears came to his mother's eyes, but she only said,

gently, "We did what we thought was for your good; I am sorry if we have made a mistake."

This melted Horace at once, and he said impetuously, "Please forgive me, mother, for speaking so; but you can't tell how this affair has worried me, and how I want you and father to know the whole truth about it; and then, O dear, I do feel so cross and ugly it's much as I can do to speak decently to anybody. But it *is* too bad to speak so to you! — how pale you look!"

"We have had a very anxious time about you, Horace; we thought at one time we must part with you; roses," she added, with a sweet smile, "do not flourish if the atmosphere is too cloudy and damp; for the rest, I know pretty well how you feel, but you must try and keep the crossness down when you can."

"O, I try hard enough; I feel mad every day when my dinner comes up, I'm so hungry and you allowance me. I could eat all the world up."

"I dare say you think you could, and I am sorry that you must be allowanced at present. Remember the second plate of broth last week, and the three days of high fever that ensued."

"O," said Horace with a grimace, "I *know* you're all right, mother dear; but for all that, 'Oliver wants more.'"

"Poor Oliver," said his mother, patting his pale,

thin cheek, " he shall have more as soon and as fast as it is safe for him."

When Mr. Grey came home and was informed of the state of Horace's feelings, he told him all that he knew about the map as concisely as possible."

" Too bad — too mean — was n't it, father?" was his comment.

" Yes, bad enough and mean enough; but worse for Van than for you."

" Did Van keep the books after he was expelled?"

" Yes; or rather Mr. Whitmore did. Van sent them back to Mr. Marsh with a saucy message, of which he took no notice, but returned them to Van's father, with the request that he would retain them for his son as a reminder of what had occurred. Mr. Whitmore was so angry with Van that he kept the books, though Van swore that he would cut them to pieces. He is to be sent to Pennsylvania, to a school where he will be under constant restriction and guardianship. I hope it is not too late to reform him from his wild courses."

" Well, father," said Horace, with a sigh of relief, " you see I was not disobedient — at least wilfully so."

" Yes, Horace, I see you have been far more sinned against than sinning; and I feel that you have had a severe lesson upon dilatory and careless habits. It may however, severe as it has been, be of the greatest service to you in the future. I could scarcely enumerate to you the evils which follow in the train of procrastination and carelessness. Many and many a man has had his life's happiness and his prosperity marred, if not totally wrecked, by indulgence in them. And they are so often considered little faults. And how often have I heard parents and friends say of boys and girls who had such faults, 'O, they are natural to childhood, — they will outgrow them.' Sometimes they do, but oftener they remain too deeply rooted in the character for any future efforts to eradicate entirely. So, my boy, while I grieve that you should thus early in life have had such a hard lesson to learn, I still think it will be a lasting benefit to you."

"I know it will, **Sir**; I have thought so much of those **little delays** and neglects that prevented me from attending to my duties; they seemed so little at the time, I never could believe they would do me so much harm. But I don't see as I was to blame for being deceived by the boys, was I?"

"**Not exactly to blame,** as I count it always nobler **to trust** than to suspect; but careless, perhaps, as I think both Stephen and Herbert warned you of them."

"Yes, I see, I was ready enough to believe in them because I wanted to, I suppose; I had such good times with them, they were so spirited and up to fun. O, dear." Then after a moment's pause, he asked, "What of Hal and Court?"

"Both doing well. Hal was heartily ashamed of his part when he saw clearly what he had been doing. He was blinded at the time by the indulgence of his revengeful feelings. Now he is doing his best to make reparation, and wishes to see you as soon as you are able to have an interview with him. As for Court, he has little real nobleness of character, and less strength. He is one of those unfortunate boys who, I fear, will always be controlled by circumstances. If favorable for the development of good, he will be negatively good; if exposed to evil influence, he will be positively base. He is under Steve's influence now, and is doing well. Steve feels that he did wrong not to watch more carefully over you, as he was older and knew the boys' character so well."

"May I see my map, father?"

"Do you think it best, — are you not already quite excited enough about it?"

"I should like to get it off my mind and have pleasant things to think of, instead of imagining how it looks."

Mr. Grey made no farther objection, but brought the map to Horace. He doubted the wisdom of the act, however, when he saw his cheeks flush crimson, and his eyes fill with tears, which, after a vain effort to repress, he suffered to flow freely; then dashing his hand across his face he said, "What a baby I am."

"Not at all, Horace. I do not wonder at your

feeling; but the thing is over now, and every one knows those careless words were not written by your hand, or those blots made by you; and Mr. Marsh intends to have another trial when you are well."

"But I shall never feel the same pleasure in doing another. It seems as if I traced in true and loyal thoughts, with every line I made on this map, and as if the resolutions that seemed to spring unbidden to my mind when I worked upon it were inscribed there. I can never have *such* feelings again.

"Perhaps not, my dear boy, just such feelings; but you may have even nobler ones. I believe our highest resolves and noblest impulses to right, in youth as well as manhood, are born of disappointment and trial when bravely met and endured as this has surely been by you. But no more talking now. You are weary and must rest."

From the date of this conversation, Horace's improvement was much more rapid. His spirits were better,—he was even tolerably good natured,—and he told his mother his greatest trial was the want of enough to eat; even that grievance was now removed, as permission was given him to satisfy his appetite as soon as he was able to exercise in the open air.

Upon his return to school he was treated with a degree of respect and regard by his schoolfellows, and consideration by Mr. Marsh, that was very gratifying to his feelings. In the second trial for the prize for the map he was entirely successful, and received a handsomely-bound edition of Longfellow's Poems.

CHAPTER XIX.

"LIGHTS AND SHADOWS."

I PASS over more than a year in the life of Mr. Grey's family, with only a slight summary of the events which occurred in that time.

Mr. and Mrs. Grey never tired in their loyal zeal for the cause of their country; and though they mourned over reverses and defeats, and sympathized with those whose dear ones had been taken from them, yet their faith in the ultimate triumph of truth and right never wavered, and their labors never slackened.

Miss St. John was happier in her life of hospital service than she had ever been in her life before, and found in it, as Mr. Grey had predicted, full scope for her energies, and for the exercise of the more than ordinary self-control and heroism which distinguished her. She had been in various situations, in temporary hospitals on the field, in cities, and on boats on the Western rivers, because she was one of those cool, resolute women who are equal to almost any emergency, and hence was called upon to fill difficult positions. The amount of good she had done in binding up bodily wounds, and pouring in the oil and wine of consolation and hope to bruised and wearied spirits, could never be estimated. At the present date of my story (May, '62,) she was in one of the hospitals in Alexandria, taking a partial rest from her labors, that she might be fit to meet the next loud call for her aid.

Margaret, too, did what she could; **and it is surprising** how much a school-girl can accomplish, in addition to daily duties **and** lessons by gathering up and using the odd moments of time, which too many consider too insignificant to be employed at all. Such forget that

> "Little drops of water,
> Little grains of sand,
> Make the mighty ocean
> And the beauteous land."

By using the odd moments, Margaret accomplished **a** good deal in the way of knitting, sewing, and making fancy articles for juvenile fairs.

As for St. John, he was the true martyr of the family for his country's service. All the others found pleasure in the work they engaged in, not only in the work itself, but in seeing its results as labors in behalf of a suffering country. He had no such satisfaction. He disliked his occupation of clerk with all the depth of decided feelings and the intensity of a strong will. Still, he never wavered nor faltered, and day after day found him at his post. If he sometimes sighed heavily for his loved books, it was in the solitude of his own room, and none of the family knew the sacrifice he was making. Could they have foreseen the extent of that sacrifice, it would never have been permitted. The spring of '62 found him so exhausted from the winter's labor, that he was obliged to keep his agreement with his father, and allow him to find a substitute for him. Contrary to all expectation, release from work did not bring with it restored health. Instead, as soon as the stimulus of necessary exertion was removed, it was seen how feeble he really was, and a slight cough gave cause for the most serious apprehensions in regard to him.

To Horace the time that had elapsed since we left him recovering from his fever had been a period of great improvement. He had given himself up to the duties of school as eagerly as heretofore he had entered into schemes for fun and enterprise, though the latter were by no means neglected. On the contrary, firm in the resolve to enter the army as soon as his parents would permit him to do so, he spent most of his lawful leisure in riding, boating, walking, and climbing, and every sport which would be most likely to develop his muscles and strengthen his body. His schoolmates had so little sympathy with the excess to which he carried his hobby, as they termed it, that they gave him the nickname of "One

Idea," which finally degenerated into "Old Idee," with a marked emphasis upon the last syllable. He could afford to be laughed at, however, for he was a tall, manly-looking fellow, with a breadth of chest to match his height, an arm whose well-developed muscle commanded respect in all athletic sports, and a countenance radiant and fresh with the health and vigor breathed in with the free air of heaven. In fact, so full of life and energy was he that his mother laughingly said it was well her young giant could spend some of his superabundant spirits elsewhere than in the house. He tormented Margaret after a different fashion now from that of his earlier years. For instance, she would be sitting by an open window, busy at her work, and, before any sign had been given of the approach of an enemy, she would find herself gently but firmly lifted from her seat, and carried to a dark room, and placed upon a lounge, from whence she was released only on declaring herself a true and loyal servant of her country. Or she would be quietly walking in the garden, and suddenly strong arms would uplift her to some high perch, where she would be kept till she had agreed to some absurd plan of Horace's, which he would gravely declare was essential to the welfare of the good cause. Or, again, she would, if walking by the river-side, be seized as a Rebel spy, placed in a boat, and rowed off to some distance from the shore, and compelled to give up her " papers" and pocket-book, which were at once pronounced "contraband." However, she never failed to find them untouched in her own room, for Horace was honorable even in his mischief.

But it was the strangest mixture of the ludicrous and pathetic — the pathetic triumphing, however, usually — to see his attempts to be quiet, and not jar upon St. John's sensitive nerves, after he was confined to the house from his sickness. His efforts to step quietly, and not make a noise, generally ended in stumbling over a footstool or small chair, knocking books off tables, or upsetting vases, which disasters he would remedy with various grimaces and expressions of sorrow, and then seat himself near St. John with a tender, wistful longing in his eyes, as if he desired to give to him some of his own overflowing life. He would try to tone down his harsh, changing voice, and talk about Thornton, and tell his pale, languid brother any little event which he thought might interest him. Then he would start up, and say, "No wonder you're pale breathing this stifled atmosphere; I must be off for one breath of air." Ah! he knew not that the chill wind of May which was life to him was torture and danger to his brother.

But I leave the family at home, with their labors of love and mercy, their absorbing young life, and their failing strength, their hopes and fears, their prayers and agonies, to return to our soldier boy, and see what time and circumstances have done for him.

Thornton had gone through almost every variety of experience that this great war affords, with the exception of any serious wound or any imprisonment more tedious and ignoble than the one recounted some chapters back. We already know in part the horrors and terrors of his first battle, and we have followed him in his inactive camp life, his foraging expeditions, his service on picket, and his daring and romantic adventure with Lee Waters. Later than that, however, commenced the real hardships of his soldier's career. He had been out upon expeditions which required long forced marches, the end of which was quite as likely to be marks of an escaped foe as anything else; and when he, with others, gladly accepted a bed of mud or the yielding morass, from utter inability to seek elsewhere for better lodgment. He had dug in trenches and aided in erecting breastworks as cheerily and as diligently as any. He had waded through mud and morass, and crossed rivers, in ordinary times deemed impassable. He had known what it was when the supply trains were temporarily cut off, to suffer from hunger and to long for a morsel of hard tack, as the traveller longs for water in the desert. He had been cold, ragged, and dirty. He had bandied jokes with his comrades upon the dignity of being ranked with the "Great Unwashed," and had proposed they should institute a

new order called "The Knights of the Ragged
Blues." And there had been times, too, though
these were comparatively few, when the joke and
laugh would not pass round, and he and others bore
silently, but unflinchingly, the hardships to which
there seemed little prospect of a speedy termination.
For soldiers engaged in active service in this wonder-
ful as well as dreadful war, could not console themselves with a newspaper paragraph, which prophesied
that this or that victory achieved, the decisive battles
of the war would be over, and a way opened to
peace. They could not so console themselves, for
they were in the enemy's country, daily, almost
hourly, meeting fresh proofs of the force, the determination, the bravery of their foe, the entire sacrifice
of every thing to the cause in which that enemy had
engaged; and they knew that many and many a
bloody battle must be fought, and many a great victory gained, before his proud heart could be subdued,
and that Rebellion, if put down in one corner of this
great land, would spring up elsewhere hydra-headed.

Thornton had followed McClellan to the peninsula
and shared with others in all the hardships that march
involved, and he had been engaged in the seven days'
fight which ensued upon their masterly retreat therefrom. And, though feeling, with others, the bitter
disappointment of the result of that campaign, he
was not discouraged or disheartened, for through all
the thick clouds that overshadowed him at times, he

knew that beyond his vision the sun of liberty was still shining, and would one day burst in full and perfect radiance upon his view. The following extract from a letter, from the colonel of his regiment to his father, will give an idea of the estimation in which he was held by his superior officer : —

"Your boy is a great credit to our regiment; cool, unflinching, in the hour of wildest excitement; never rash or headlong, his example has been of infinite service to the other boys in his company; not alone in the respects I have mentioned, but also in his perfectly proper and soldier-like deference to his superior officers. At first, many of our free and independent 'sovereigns' in the army found it very galling to conform to military etiquette and subordination to those with whom they had formerly been 'hale fellows well met.' But Thornton and a few more like him, have set noble examples, and thus have influenced hundreds. I can hardly tell the mischief that would have ensued if he and others of his social position in life had shown any distaste to conforming to rules and obeying orders. And this influence has been gained not by any assumption of condescension, but simply by doing their duty as an entire matter of course. Long ago I would have recommended your boy for promotion, but he did not wish it. 'No, sir,' he said to me, 'let me earn promotion by two years service in the ranks; then, if my superior officers are satisfied that I deserve it, I will gladly accept it.'

The two years are out, and he will soon receive a lieutenant's commission, and I doubt not he will rise rapidly.

"Another respect in which his example has been of great service in his company, is the uniformly fair and generous treatment he has shown towards the Rebels with whom the fortunes of war have brought him in contact, thereby commanding their respect and obliging them to alter their notions of the Yankee character. It is true the necessities of our situation have obliged him at times to join foraging expeditions, but I have been told his influence has always been exerted to protect those from whom these unwilling contributions have been levied, from wanton injury and insult. In conclusion, my dear sir, let me say that this war has made a man of your son; a consistent, brave, and noble-hearted man, too; and, that living or dying for his country, you have every reason to be proud of him; proud with a true Christian pride. For the sake of our long friendship I have watched him narrowly, and I am conscious he is turning the circumstances of his situation to the best account. I wish I could say as much for poor Ned Howe, who is falling as low as your son is rising high in the esteem of others. It is probable his commission will be taken from him."

When this letter was read aloud in the family circle, it was received by Horace with noisy demonstrations of delight. "Hurrah for my brother, the lieutenant that is to be! Good for old Sleepy Hollow! He did n't sleep in those old days for nothing. When he's promoted I'll step into his shoes as private. I'm as big and strong as he was when he left. Say yes, father? All right, silence gives consent. Here, Mag, let's have a waltz in honor of my brother, the lieutenant. What, crying? the dickens, how solemn you all look! I should think Thorny had been shot instead of promoted. Come, Cæsar, let's ventilate our feelings in the woods, old boy."

And off started boy and dog, apparently in the highest spirits; but they were no sooner out of sight than Horace threw himself upon the grass, gave a deep sigh, which ended in a quick sob, and exclaimed, "O, dear, what a fool I always am, to make such a noise, and St. John so sick. I *know* he thinks he shall never see Thornton again, and they are so fond of each other!"

CHAPTER XX.

"Poor Ned" and the Babes in the Wood.

In Camp, June, '63.

About this matter of promotion, which elates you so much, Horace, I must confess I feel not a little gratified at having earned my honors, much more so than if I had received the commission, long ago, simply because I was my father's son. My comrades in arms are as glad for me as I am for myself, although I am younger than many of them who are not promoted. It is pleasant, too, to stay on in the old regiment. My predecessor was obliged to return home on account of sickness, and I just step into his place. My heartiest congratulations have been from Holdfast, now corporal, and Pat.

Holdfast, with a grip of the hand that almost made me wince, said, "I've only one fault to find with them that gin ye yer commission, and that is, that they didn't turn out the cap'n neck and heels and put ye in his place. Thunder and lightnin'! but I call it a pesky shame to put honest men under a chap who doesn't know half the time whether he's on his head or his heels. I'll be blamed ef I don't 'bleve he'll come to grief yit, and that of the worst sort, at the hands of some of the men. They hate him tarnation bad. Now, we all on us feel respect and so on for ye, and would go to the devil ef ye bade us, an' think ye had a reason for it."

"Thank you for your good will and good faith, Holdfast," said I. "I should n't like to test it in the way you speak of, however. I'm sorry for the captain. He means to do right, but he is easily tempted. At all events, I don't want his place."

"O yis, he means to do right p'raps, but I guess his resolutions is the kind of commodity that hell's paved with; in that case they ain't likely to do him nor us a tarnation sight of good. Mark my words, he's got bitter enemies, an' he'll git come up with yit."

"Surely, Holdfast, if you know of any plot against him, you ought to make it known."

"I don' know any plots agin him, I only know he's all-fired unpopular, an' I know there's boys in our company that as lief shoot him as a Rebel, in fact a heap sooner."

"Can nothing be done, the idea is dreadful."

"*I* don' know how you kin *do* nothin' when you don' *know* nothin'. I never heerd anybody say they'd like to shoot him, though I've seen 'em look it afore now. Yer an officer now, yer might gin him some good advice; if it warn't nothin' but pourin' water into a sieve, 't wouldn't be your fault. But I was arter congratulating you, which I does most heartily; ef ever a man or boy desarved promotion you's the chap; beg pardon, lieutenant, for the liberty I takes, I forgits old times is done."

"Old times never will be done for you and me in this world, old fellow," I said, heartily grasping his big rough hand. "We'll hold fast to each other to the death, as good friends and true, and after death too, as I hope and believe."

"That's so," he said, with a queer twinkle in his grey eyes, "I'm agreeable ef you be. I allers knowed you was one of the true quality. Them's the sort I'd as lief take off my hat to as not ef I kin remember it; but when it comes to yer whippersniffers, and dandies, and monkeys, I just 'spise 'em." (Perhaps, Horace, you can define whipper-sniffers, I can't.)

Just then up comes Pat with "the top of the morning to yer honor. May yees live a thousand years and die a major-gineral in the prime of yer life, with all yer forefathers around yees. And it's meself that'll say I knowed yees when ye was nothin' but a private that riz by raison of yer merits."

"I thanked Pat for his rather Irish wishes, and I cannot help being amused at the evident pride he takes in my promotion, apparently considering it as a personal compliment."

After my chat with Holdfast, I sought an opportunity to speak with Ned Howe. I found him alone in his quarters one evening, his head resting on both hands in a state of great depression. "What is the matter, Ned?" I asked, as cheerily as possible. When we are by ourselves we dispense with formalities.

"Matter enough, as nobody knows better than yourself," he answered, gruffly enough; then added, "Oh, Thornton, the devil's got me soul and body; it's no use contending."

"Not so, Ned; 'never too late to mend,' you know. Put your will to the work of reform; strive, pray, and you'll find you have no devil that cannot be exorcised."

"I have tried and tried; as for praying, it don't come natural to me."

"I should think it would come natural to any one who feels as keenly as you do the weakness of your own resolutions. You have everything at stake, and more than that Ned, your course is making you excessively unpopular in the company; with some even to a dangerous extent."

"I know it, said he, doggedly; I've seen it in their black scowling faces. I hope the next fight'll end it all."

"But think of your mother, Ned," I said, " and of your friends at home."

"My mother!" he answered with a fearful oath, "if she had been a true mother to me I should never have had this fatal habit. Who encouraged me to sip wine after dinner and laughed at my first tipsy speeches, and thought it was pretty? Who, when I was older and carried out the taste she had fostered, and came home drunk, — yes, drunk; it's a coarse word to use, but a coarser thing to do, — spurned me from her with disgust, and was too much absorbed in her round of pleasures to try and win me back to right?"

"Still, you had every inducement to reform when you joined the army, and were placed in such a responsible situation, and I don't think it quite right when a man is of age to judge between good and evil, to charge one's faults or follies upon others."

"No it isn't right, I suppose, but I have bitter feelings towards my mother; she seems so willing I should go down, down. To be sure, there's poor little Lina, it's hard for her."

"For your sister's sake, then Ned, for your country's sake, for the sake of all that is best and noblest in your nature, do try and give up this habit."

"I'm bound hand and foot, a perfect slave to the habit, as *you* call it, to the *demon*, as I call it. I haven't your strength of mind. You could go to the stake like the martyrs of old, while I should recant again and again. I'm not of the stuff to resist temptation as you do, and make it a means of improvement. No, I say again, I hope the next fight — and it'll be a tough one — will finish me. I'm tired of living. A good thing for you, you'll get my place; and you'll do it honor, too."

Poor, poor Ned; he looked so despairing that I almost felt as if his words were prophetic. I found he did n't wish to talk any more, so I left him with a cordial grasp of the hand and the words, " do try hard, for Lina's sake."

It is dreadful to see him so hopeless, and dreadful to hear him blame his mother for his vice. Yet who knows how far he is responsible for faults that arise from early neglect. I can't judge; only this I know, conscience speaks ever, if parents do not. God has given us one sure guide, if we will heed it.

You ask me about the other boys, Horace, how they get on, &c. Dub and Brag are the two that have changed the most. There's not a trace of the mother's boy now in Dub, except such traces of truth and honor and bravery that true mothers inspire in their boys' hearts; and Mrs. Winslow's soothing syrup is at a discount. He can go unwashed and uncombed with as good a grace as the best, drop down in the mud for a night's lodging, and joke about our old order as heartily as any of us; and he's all pluck and nerve.

As for Brag, though sometimes a little nervous, he never shrinks from any duty, however exposed, and now acts his courage, whereas before he talked it. His place is more than filled, though, by a couple of recruits that have been in service only a few months. These boys, a couple of big six-footers, with bone and muscle enough to beat a score of us, are the most arrant cowards that ever tried to pull a trigger. They get well tormented, you may be sure, and Pat gave them a name that stuck to them till some one found another. We were engaged one day in a skirmish with an unseen foe,— that is, we were on a plain and the Rebs in a wood near by, and the shots they sent out to us were rather more sure of a mark than ours, fired at hap-hazard. One of these brave boys had a trick of clapping his cartridge-box up to the side of his head every time a bullet whizzed by, and always on the wrong side. Presently a bullet came that nearly took off a bit of his ear. Such a howl as he set up, his friend joining in, and they both commenced a series of hops unlike any figure I ever saw performed in the dancing-hall or on the battle-field.

"Me faith," said Pat, "do ye see the big grasshoppers out yonder? Barring there's no grass here, it makes one think of the warrum summer time, it does."

This occurred some weeks ago, and the name clung to those valiant youths till Jim gave them another. Poor Jim, he seldom gets off any witticisms nowadays, for his wound injured his health seriously. He ought to be at home under treatment, but he says he would rather live two years for his country than forty for himself. But I was to tell you of the second adventure of our "grasshoppers." This time the enemy were opposite us on a rising ground, while we were upon a flat, and a small river between. They had so manifest an advantage over us that we were ordered to lie down and do what we could in the way of returning their deadly attentions in that position. It was near dark, and we soon got tired of fighting in that fashion, and begged to be allowed "to give it to 'em" once upon our feet. So, loading, we rose with a shout that might of itself have frightened a common foe, so shrilly did it ring out upon the air. If the cry did n't frighten them our unexpected shot did, and we were able to repeat it before they got well over their astonishment. We outnumbered them, and after the proof we had given of our intentions they withdrew, with the design, we thought, of inducing us to cross the river and follow them. We suspected they wanted to get us into an ambush, as we knew a large body of their forces was encamped not far distant, — so we remained where we were, keeping close watch lest we should be surprised, intending to rejoin our regiment in the morning. We missed our "grasshoppers," and upon inquiring one of the men said he had seen them making tracks for the wood behind us soon after we had risen to our feet.

"O ho!" said Jim; "Babes in the Wood, are they? Wonder if the robins will cover the dears with leaves, to keep them warm? Come, Thorn, it 's our duty to look them up."

We went into the wood, and soon found them, —

one sitting upon the ground holding the head of his comrade, and both of them chattering with cold, or fear, or both.

They took us for the enemy, and cried for mercy in the most abject tones. Jim proposed to me, in a whisper, that we should follow out the idea, and pretend to take them prisoners.

"No," said I. "In the first place you might frighten the fools to death; in the second, I've no patience to joke with such craven-hearted creatures."

So I stepped up to them and asked them sternly what they were doing there, while we had been fighting.

"O," said the one who was sitting down, "that's you, is it, Private Grey? John, here, has had an awful wound, and I came with him to stop the bleeding. He's been awful faint, John has, and I thought he was gone once."

"Let me see it."

With much preliminary caution, and, I fancy, some inward misgiving, the man unbound a handkerchief from the arm of his still groaning comrade.

"Pooh," said Jim; "a mere scratch — a flesh-wound, which a couple of ——"

"O, it wasn't the wound alone; it was the effect of the bleeding. He told me he had been subject to fits from an infant, brought on by the loss of blood."

"Haw, haw, haw!" roared Jim; "I don't doubt it. Fits, indeed! Yes, that's the plain truth; nobody doubts that story."

"Come," said I, angrily, "we've had enough of this nonsense; come with us."

"Are — they — all — gone, — are you quite sure?" asked the man of fits.

"Who gone, — the Rebs or our fellows?" inquired Jim.

"Oh, the Rebels. You didn't see em as we did, — there was a lot on 'em."

"Yes, they're gone to bring up reinforcements, probably; about time for them to be back. I don't know but our boys have gone too. I left them debating the matter," said Jim, with unblushing effrontery.

They both found their feet with astonishing celerity, and exclaimed in concert, "Gone, and left us to our fate!"

"Why not?" said Jim; "if they *have* gone, and I don't say as they have, of course they thought you would keep guard, and let us know if the enemy was coming."

When we rejoined our Company many were the inquiries made as to the nature of the wounds the missing men had received, and Jim's account was listened to with roars of laughter.

"The Babes in the Wood, boys, — the latest edition issued; tender, innocent creatures. I commend them to your care, as the robins are all asleep, particularly this unfortunate babe, who is subject to fits; speak gently to him, nurse him tenderly."

Jim was interrupted by the appearance of our Captain, who was perfectly sober, but in an exceedingly irritable mood. "What's all this noise, boys? I should think you had better be sleeping; you'll have to fight to-morrow."

Jim related the adventure again in his comical way, but the Captain swore furiously if ever such a thing happened again the men should be reported as deserters. And so the affair ended, only they still go by the name of the Babes in the Wood, and are obliged to listen to all sorts of changes rung upon the story. Perhaps this seems flat to you, — it is ludicrous enough to us, with all the accompaniments of comical looks and the aspect of the men when they receive the hits, which come hard sometimes. They try to keep it off, for they do not dare to resent it; but, as Jim says, they laugh the wrong side of the mouth. But cowards and sneaks are, I am happy to say, the exception. Aside from the benefit this experience of a soldier's life in the rank and file has been to me, I shall always feel more kindly towards my fellow-men in consequence of it. I told you before that shams of any sort don't go down in camp life. You see men as they are when the restraints of home and society are removed, and they sit with you by the camp fire or join you on the long march. And you often find among those from whom you would least expect it, traits of self-denial and nobleness which gladdens your heart and makes you feel more than ever that goodness and greatness are not confined to any favored portion of society. These acts, too, are such as will never be blazoned abroad, although they will be forever enshrined in the hearts of their comrades. To everything in life there is a reverse side, and brutality, coarseness, and profanity are found also, but I believe in less proportion than the redeeming traits.

But I have wandered away from my subject, which was to tell you of my companions in arms. This leaf in my journal is like some of the figures I learned at dancing school, where various evolutions to the right, left, and front, bring you back to the point whence you started. I am back now to Lee Waters, of whom I know you wish to hear. He has changed somewhat since you last met him in his romantic adventure with Emily. He is in better health, more cheerful, and a little less vindictive than of old, though still far enough from being what I call a model soldier. Model he is for bravery and endurance, but he still fights the Rebels more as personal enemies than as enemies of his country.

News has just been received that the enemy are in considerable force in Pennsylvania, and we are ready for marching at an hour's notice. From all we can gather this is not a mere raid to seize supplies, &c.; but is intended to be a great victory over us upon our own soil. We are ready, whatever comes; and I, for one, feel a firm conviction that we are to conquer the Rebels this time, — with heavy loss it may be, but Victory, Victory is our watchword.

If I should fall, remember, Horace, that I have never for one moment regretted that I enlisted, and that I die willingly for my country, nay gladly, if the sacrifice is needed. And as I feel so feel thousands of others in our army. If it does sound like self-glorification (though I speak not for myself, I know, but as if I stood apart), I say, All honor to the rank and file of the armies of the United States! The country will never know how many thousands of brave, untitled martyrs have suffered and died that she might live, and that forever —

"The star-spangled banner triumphant shall wave,
  O'er the land of the free and the home of the brave."

But God knows, and he will reward each one according to his deeds, be he high or low private, master or servant.

Good night, Horace. I have a strange feeling that I shall perhaps never take pen in hand more, and yet I do not feel that I shall die yet. If I do, still remember I die willingly.

CHAPTER XXI.

GETTYSBURG AND THE HOSPITAL.

You all know how bravely the battle of Gettysburg was fought, and that it resulted in a total rout of the self-confident Rebels, and a complete victory for our troops, and that simultaneously with the shouts of victory went up the wail of mourning for the loved and slain upon the battle-field.

The regiment to which Thornton belonged bravely did their share of the three days' fighting, and came out of the conflict with the loss of nearly one half in killed and wounded. Among the former were the Captain, Corporal Trim, Pat, and Brag. Among the latter Thornton and Lee Waters, Holdfast and Dub. There were dark rumors afloat that the Captain's death was caused by a bullet from one of his own men, but there had been no time for investigation. Corporal Trim had escaped wonderfully, for he was brave as a lion, till the close of the third day, when he fell, shot through the heart with a bullet. Pat had risked and lost his life in an excited rush after a tall Rebel, against whom he had been observed to have an especial spite. His earnestness had carried him too far into the enemy's ranks, and he had fallen pierced through and through with bullets. Brag had done nobly, and had proved himself a true hero at last; for he had rushed to the aid of the color-bearer, who was in imminent danger, and had been shot down in defence of the flag of his country.

Thornton had received a wound in his face which had bled profusely, and which promised to disfigure his mouth forever. In addition to that, he had a severe wound in his thigh, a slighter one in his right side, and his right leg had been trampled upon and severely bruised, for he had lain long upon the field unconscious of all that was transpiring around him.

Lee Waters and Holdfast were also badly, but not dangerously wounded; and Dub was positively jubilant over the loss of his left arm. Poor fellow, he thought the glory of it was more than a compensation for his loss.

When Thornton recovered his senses he found his Aunt Esther bending over him, with a kindly look upon her face and a moisture in her eyes such as he had never seen there before. Faint and bewildered, he murmured, "Thank God, I am at home. Where is mother?" and then closed his eyes again in exhaustion. He was in one of the many quickly improvised hospitals in Gettysburg, and his Aunt Esther had come at once to the battle-ground to look after him; and through her exertions he had been discovered among the slain and wounded. For a few days Thornton's life trembled in the balance, and his father and mother and Miss St. John watched over him with unceasing anxiety. At the expiration of that time the surgeon said he would live if nothing unforseen occurred to retard his recovery, but that it would be many weeks before he could go into service again. As soon as he was out of danger Mrs. Grey returned home to St. John, whose failing health demanded all her loving care. Previous to doing so, however, she had a conversation with Thornton about his brother. Up to this time, and while there had been a shadow of hope that he might recover, Thornton had been kept in ignorance of his real condition. It was now thought best to prepare him for the shock of meeting St. John. When his mother told him she must go home, Thornton asked: "Must you leave me, mother? I think I can travel in a few days, and I shall miss you *so* much, though, to be sure, Aunt Esther is a capital nurse."

"Yes, I must go, my son; St. John needs me."

"What is the matter with St. John, mother? I know he is n't well, but you seem so anxious whenever you speak of him; is it anything more than debility caused by over-exertion?"

"We hoped it was nothing more for a long time, but now his symptoms only too clearly indicate the steady progress of a fatal disease. I tell you this, Thornton, for I think you will bear it bravely, and not suffer the sad intelligence to injure you or retard your recovery."

"Oh, mother, can it be?" was all Thornton could say for some moments, then he added, "why could not I have been taken and he spared?"

"Because," said Mrs. Grey, with tearful eyes and trembling lips, "such was not God's will. You must fill a double place when —— when he is gone. When you return to us you will, I know, strive to be cheerful; he will wish it."

"Does he know, is he ready and willing? Oh, mother, it cannot be. There was so much he had planned to do; he was so earnest in all he ever undertook, earnest and faithful! *I* take St. John's place to you? never; I am hardly worthy to be his brother."

"I do not wonder that you feel as you do, Thorny. I have often felt rebuked in his presence. I think he is aware of his situation; but he hasn't seemed disposed to talk of himself. I fear he has had a hard struggle. When I return to him he will no doubt talk freely to me. Do not dwell too sadly upon this impending sorrow. God doeth all things well, and out of great peril He has saved you to comfort us."

"I was going to ask a favor of you, mother, but now I think I ought not."

"Ask it, my boy, and I will freely grant it, if it is in my power."

"I wanted to ask if you would invite Holdfast

and Lee Waters to pass a few weeks with us till they are quite fit for service. Lee has no friends to whom he can go, and Holdfast is too far from his to go home. But it is not right to trouble you now, that you have St. John to take care of."

Mrs. Grey thought a few moments and then answered, "I think it will be a good thing for us all. It will interest St. John, too. I know nothing would give him more pleasure. We have pleasant rooms, good servants, and everything needed to make them comfortable. Your father will be glad to have them come. By all means ask them, Thorny. If St. John becomes alarmingly sick, it will only be needful to keep his rooms quiet."

"But, mother!"

"What is it, now, Thorny?"

"Will *you* ask them? Lee is very proud and sensitive. I am afraid I should n't ask him in the right way, and as for Holdfast, it would please him so much to have you invite him."

"With pleasure, I will do it at once."

Mrs. Grey passed out of the room, and seeking her husband, told him of Thornton's wishes, and her readiness to gratify them, adding, she was sure of his approval.

"Certainly, if you wish it; nothing could be more gratifying to me. I have thought of it, but I did not know but it would be too much for you. My heart has ached many a time for poor homeless fellows. The least we can do is to open our doors to them."

When Mrs. Grey, taking in her own, Lee's hot, wasted hand, said gently and tenderly, in sweet motherly tones, "I have a favor to ask of you, my dear young friend," he looked up amazed, and said, "a favor to ask of me? I do not know how I can do anything for you, but you have only to ask it; I should be most ungrateful to refuse you anything."

"Then come home with Thornton for a rest, and remain till you are fit to go to the army again. My son tells me you have a friend not far from us. It will be very gratifying to her to be able to visit you often. I have an invalid son whose whole heart is enlisted for our soldiers. It will beguile many a weary hour for him if you will come."

Lee flushed scarlet, and said, "I cannot grant you a favor, for it is all on my side, but I will thankfully go to your home. I do not deserve it, though. I am not like Thornton."

"If you consent we will not talk about the matter, or decide whose obligation is the greater. I must gladden Thornton by telling him you will go; he wishes it so much."

As Mrs. Grey approached the cot upon which Holdfast lay, the surgeon was just leaving him. He greeted Mrs. Grey with the words, "I am glad to see you. I hope you bring an antidote for the unwelcome sentence I have just passed upon our sturdy friend."

"Yes, marm," said Holdfast, with an odd grimace, "I need some sort 'o sugar-plums arter bein' told I could n't use this pesky arm for six weeks. What's a feller to do idling about all that time?"

"I've come just in season then to tell you," said Mrs. Grey, kindly, shaking his left hand (the right arm was the one disabled).

"Go with my son and breathe the pure air of our country home. It will be next to the pine woods in Maine. Thornton wishes it very much, and Mr. Grey and myself also. My youngest son will hardly leave you a moment's peace, so anxious will he be to hear your fortunes in war. It will gratify us all if you will consent."

"Waall, I never heerd the like of this; you really want me to go to your home; *me*, such a rough-spoken chap 's I be? Thunder and lightnin'! guess I 'm delirious."

"I guess not," said Mrs. Grey with a smile, softly laying her hand upon his forehead. "No, not a bit; shall I tell Thorny you 'll come? He has quite set his heart upon it."

"Shall I go to paradise when I git 'a chance, or stay out in the cold and dark? that 's 'bout it; thank ye, marm. Guess I 'll go to paradise, seein' 's your so good 's to ax me. Waall, I allers did think Thornton Grey must 'a had a powerful good bringin' up, and now I 's sure on it." Then changing his tone of astonishment to one of deep feeling, and wiping away some suspicious moisture with the back of his hand, he said, "God bless you, marm, for the thought. I shall be a better man all my days for your goodness."

"Thank you, cordially, for consenting to come. Horace will try and make it as pleasant to you as possible, I know, and we shall feel proud to have three of the heroes of Gettysburg at once under our roof."

Holdfast followed Mrs. Grey as long as he could with his eyes, and then muttered to himself, "Waall, I never; makin' a favor on it, too, to herself and family. Hope 't ain't a dream; allers thought should like ter know ef the gentry had hearts like common folks. Some on 'em has, that's so."

"Aunt Esther," said Thornton, one day, to that lady, after she had bound up his wounds, and carefully adjusted his pillow to suit him, "I'm getting jealous."

"Of whom, pray?" was the response.

"That's just what I want you to tell me, *who* the chap is, you are so devoted to the other side of the room. Such care as *he* gets; such nice things as you take him; such talks as you have with him; such words of comfort as you read to him. If I did n't know you on your own telling for a 'cross-grained old maid,' I should think you had some wounded colonel, of suitable years, whose gallant deeds and wounds, 'poor dumb mouths,' had at last touched your hardest of hard hearts!"

"Will nothing ever take the nonsense out of you, Thornton Grey?" replied his aunt, trying to look severe, and evidently confused at this question.

"It's only a boy, — younger than you are."

"*It* isn't an it. I suppose you meant to say *he's* only a boy."

"Well, suppose I did?"

"Suppose you tell me his name, his regiment, &c. &c. I feel a strong interest in all our boys, and I feel an especial interest in any one who interests my aunt so deeply."

"His name is Thomas Jefferson Peyton; his regiment, &c. I have n't asked. He is suffering, and has no friends to look after him. Any more questions, Mr. Inquisitive?"

"Yes, no; I reckon father 'll find out anything more I want to know."

"Your father! you need n't trouble yourself to ask him. Peyton is a Virginian, and a —— Rebel."

"Whew-ew-ew! that's a joke. 'Never, if I know my own heart, will I give aid or succor to a Rebel.' I quote from memory; do I quote correctly? To think how careful I've been not to let you know how many times I've bound up the wounds of, and given cups of cold water to, these same Rebels, lest you should doubt my patriotism, and now, to find *you* doing the same thing! Oh, auntie, you had a heart, after all, for them as for us."

"I feel just as I did about them in the mass, or

rather, I think them more wicked and ungrateful than I ever did, but I cannot help feeling interested in some of them as individuals. When you can walk, come over and see this fair-skinned, golden-haired boy, with a girl's beauty and the soul of a hero; if his cause is one that I detest, I must say I honor him. He is deceived; he believes, or did believe, all he has always been taught about us. He sees now we are not barbarians. When I first went to him to remove the bandages from his wound and put on others, I really believe he thought I was going to let him bleed to death. I soon quieted him, however, and to me he has been gentle and grateful since."

"I can readily believe it, auntie," said Thornton, laying aside his jesting manner, "and I rejoice that you are proving to him that humanity knows no distinction between friend or foe with us. Poor, poor boy, I pity him without having seen him; and as for you, aunt Esther, I always knew how kind you were at heart, and I was in earnest when I said, before I went to the war, you would nurse all who required your care, tenderly, friend or foe."

"Thank you for your just appreciation of me, Thornton. You understood me better than I understood myself."

Yes; until now Esther St. John had never fully known what a deep well of tenderness and humanity was in her heart. Some natures are never developed by the events of everyday life. It requires more than common influences to smite the rock which hold the waters back. Such influences she had found in the hospital service, and on the field of Gettysburg; the rock had been smitten, and the deep fountains of Esther St. John's heart had been opened, and its waters gushed forth full and free, carrying refreshing and healing to all within her reach, and to her own surprise she had found her heart was large enough to embrace in its compassion the Rebel as well as the loyal sufferer from the horrors of war.

Is not the unsealing of such noble natures to the world and themselves part of the silver lining of the black cloud of war?

CHAPTER XXII.

MR. GREY'S LIBRARY ONCE MORE.

It is a far different scene that we look upon, in that pleasant gathering-place of Mr. Grey's family, from the one in which we first met the three brothers. They are all there now, and it is not necessary for me to tell you that they are changed, for that you know already if you have followed the progress of this story.

Perhaps of the three the one of whom we have known the least in these pages has had the hardest battles to fight; and, judging from his countenance, his victory has been complete, and he has already entered into his reward. To a few pure spirits, who have bravely fought the good fight, and so conquered themselves as to yield with childlike love and trust to a heavenly Father's will, — to a few such God grants on earth such foretaste of the joys of heaven, that not only are their own hearts lifted up to serene heights of peace, but those who are in daily intercourse with them are sometimes privileged almost to behold the heavenly gates, and the world and its delights and temptations and sorrows are almost forgotten. Such a spirit was St. John Grey, and such was the influence he exerted over the other members of the family. Even Horace, who, in his stirring boy life and keen enjoyment of the present, knew not the need as yet of something higher and more spiritual than he had yet attained, was chastened and softened by intercourse with the brother whom he regarded with a mixture of awe and veneration, and who had already spiritually passed beyond the veil, to him.

After Mrs. Grey's return from Gettysburg, St. John had in this very room poured out to her the free confidence of his heart; and even his mother felt that his was a nature so far purified from the dross of earth, that heaven alone could henceforth satisfy his longings.

After inquiring most earnestly for Thornton, and expressing his gratitude at the prospect of his recovery, he added, "It would have been so hard, mother, for you to part with us both."

"My boy, my darling!"

"Yes, mother, you know that I must go hence. I am ready and willing, and you will not hold me back. I believe none of our brave heroes in the war have had harder battles to fight; but then I have come out of my battles healed, not wounded, renewed, not blighted; and oh, mother, do not grieve; but I wish to go, I am so weary, and I do not want to be drawn back to the world, and have to fight my battles over again. Let me go, dear mother, and do not be too sad for my loss from your bodily sight."

A gentle pressure of the hot, wasted hand she held was the only answer Mrs. Grey could give; and St. John continued: —

"Life was very dear to me, I had so many plans and hopes for the future, — how dear, with its broad field of labor and its calls for service from every true heart, none can tell; for I do not think any one can understand fully the feelings of a person who is debarred by physical infirmity from mingling in the more active pursuits of life. I think they are supposed to have less hold upon life from their very infirmities; whereas I think the contrary is often the case. From a little fellow up I have thought and planned what I should do in the future, and how, if God had given me but one talent, I would use that in his service. Few boys of my age ever have time to think seriously as I have done; hence few could have cherished schemes to forego. Since this war broke out, I have so longed, so hoped, so prayed, to be able to serve my country directly in some way. I thought, if I could not wait to be fitted to go as chaplain, I could do something in the hospitals. I know I could be of use there, for my heart would be in my work. But I soon found God's plans for me were not my plans. Oh, mother, it is such blessed peace to be able to say and to *feel*, 'Thy will be done!'"

Much more had mother and son to say to each other in this free outpouring of the heart, but I have told you enough to enable you to do justice to St. John's character, and to understand why his battles were so hard to fight, and why the victory was so complete. One more contest, however, he had with himself, and this came from a cause for which he was quite unprepared. He had entered warmly into his mother's plan for receiving Lee and Holdfast into their home, and had thanked her for it, as for a personal favor; but when they arrived, he was at first repelled by Lee's proud reserve, and by the harsh and vindictive spirit he evinced in conversation. For a few days he held himself aloof from him, and, if he talked at all, it was with Holdfast, whose sturdy, honest nature interested him at once. He soon felt, however, that this was a wrong course to pursue, injurious to himself, as well as debarring him from obtaining **any** good influence over Lee. He soon won Lee's confidence, and, when he understood how such a noble, generous nature had become soured, he set himself to minister to a mind diseased. He learned that an orphaned childhood, dependence upon unsympathizing **and** grudging relatives, premature contest with the stern, cold realities of life, **and**, lastly, his intense anxiety for Emily, the only star visible to him in his dark night of life, and indignation against her persecutors, had made him what he was.

You must not think that St. John influenced Lee by set discourses upon the duties of life, or formal scriptural teaching of the broad charity which is love, taught in the gospel. No; he knew too well that Lee would only chafe under such teaching. He repaid confidence with confidence, showed the struggles and longings of his own heart, its rebellion, its final submission, and then the fruits of that submission; and all this was done so naturally, so kindly, that before he was aware of the change, Lee felt that, to be a true soldier in battle, one must first be a soldier of the cross of Christ.

Let us now return to the assembled company in the library, for it is the night before Holdfast and Lee Waters leave to go to the army, being now quite able to perform their duties.

Thornton lies upon the lounge, his old favorite resting-place. The scar on his face will soon be hidden by his beard, and his wounds are now rapidly healing, but he still requires weeks more of home care and nursing to make him fit to encounter hardships again. Horace sits on a mat beside him, and near Holdfast, who has drawn his chair just behind Thornton's lounge. St. John reclines in an easy-chair, his face lighted up with inward peace; and on a stool at his feet sits Margaret, sometimes knitting, sometimes glancing upwards with a strange, wistful longing into St. John's face. Near by are Lee Waters and Emily Ray, for the latter has been a frequent guest at Mrs. Grey's since the return of her soldier-boy. How bright and happy, even radiant, she looks! For the joy in her heart at the change in Lee makes her almost forgetful that this is the last meeting for who knows how long a time between the two? Who knows, indeed!

As for Lee, his attention is divided between Emily and St. John. Emily is his own; he hopes to live many years blessed with her companionship. St. John he may never meet again on earth, and to St. John he owes the peace and rest, the noble enthusiasm, the true courage, and the Christian fortitude which shines out of his now really noble face. Mr. Grey sits by the table in the centre of the room, and Mrs. Grey by St. John, her hand laid lightly upon his, as it rests on the arm of the chair.

There is a hush of deep feeling over all, broken by Thornton, who says, lightly, "Beware, boys, not to rise too far above me by your deeds of valor before I return to the army. To be robbed of honors by my soldier boys would be too much even for my Sleepy-Hollowism."

"Guess the Sleepy Hollow's about played out of you," said Horace.

"I don't know about that. It's mighty easy, and natural too, to lie here and be petted. It's only the fear of being outstripped in rank that makes me anxious to return to the army."

"Very well for you to say, old hypocrite!" retorted Horace; "but I wish you would hurry up and get well, so's to get a place for me in your company. You know I'm to enlist this autumn; is n't it so, father?"

"Yes," replied Mr. Grey, "if you wish; if you think it best to do so when the proper time comes."

This was said so gravely Horace looked astounded, but made no answer. Another long pause ensued, which was broken by Holdfast so abruptly that most of the company started as if a gun had been fired off amongst them.

"'T ain't no use for me to try and make a great speech, marm; I never was no great at talkin', — doin''s my business; but I must say's I don' see how's I ever going to thank you for all yer kindness, I mean all on yer. 'T ain't so much the good food and good lodgin' you give me, though that's been fit for a prince, and by no means despised, but it's the kindness an' — an' — what I've larnt here, that's what makes me wish I *could* say what I want to; but I can't, so 'tain't no use to try."

"We never can repay our obligations to you all, Mrs. Grey," said Lee; "and I am sure I am as much at a loss to know how to express my gratitude to you as Holdfast is. His debt is nothing to mine, though. I know how I can repay it in part, and I will try to do it. I will try henceforth," he added, in a lower, solemn tone of voice, almost as if registering a vow, "to be a Christian soldier."

"Waall," said Holdfast, gathering fresh courage from this aid, " guess my debt's much the same as yourn. Anyhow, it's the first time I ever felt sartin there was suthin reel in religion. Now I've seen with my eyes, and heerd with my ears, that folks that's rich an' prosperous can pray and practice too. It'll be comfort to me nights, when I'm out in the cold an' mud an' dark, to feel sartin there's sich good folks to hum who thinks on us."

"It is the very least we can do for you, who do so much for us," said Mrs. Grey. "We are only one family among thousands and thousands who think and feel and act as we do. As for your debt to us, ours to you is far greater. I cannot express to you the real heartfelt pleasure it has been to us to have you here. Your visit has done us all good.'

"Yes," said Horace, "it has been such jolly times to hear about your scrapes, and fighting, and everything. I don't know what I shall do with myself till Thorn goes back. I want a field for my vast energies."

It was strange how many fruitless efforts were made that evening to talk. Every one felt too deeply for words, and after a few more attempts of Horace to draw out his soldier friends, Mr. Grey said, "Some of us must take an early breakfast tomorrow, and St. John looks weary. Let us unite in our usual evening service." After reading the twentieth chapter of the Gospel of John, which came in regular order for the evening reading, he turned to the twenty-seventh psalm, beginning, " The Lord is my light and my salvation; whom shall I fear? The Lord is the strength of my life; of whom shall I be afraid?" As he read this full outpouring of love and faith of the Psalmist of Israel, and especially the closing verse, in tones of deep feeling, " Wait on the Lord: be of good courage, and he shall strengthen thy heart: wait, I say, on the Lord," there was not one present who did not feel strengthened and encouraged for future hardship and trial. The prayer which followed was one of those heart utterances that strike some chord in every human breast. It was a prayer of faith and love, a fervent supplication for God's protection and fatherly care for all; alike those who remained at home in peace and comfort, and those who went forth to the perils of battle. As he concluded, Holdfast rose from his seat, held out his rough hand, which was warmly grasped by Mr. Grey, and said, " thank ye, sir," and sat down again. The act was simple and touching, for it told how completely the soldier had been taken out of himself and uplifted above all his usual shyness and awkwardness.

It was usual to close with singing, as most of the party could join and Margaret played upon the piano. " America" was proposed, but Horace begged first for " Daughter of Zion awake from thy sadness," and it was sung, all joining but Thornton, St. John, and Holdfast.

"America" followed, and then the party dispersed. Holdfast was the first to go, cordially shaking hands with Thornton, and saying, "I shall miss ye, a heap; come back soon 's yer can." To St. John's kind wishes for his welfare, he could only falter out, "There's no need for me to give ye good wishes; I reckon you've got the peace that passeth **understanding**. I'll never, never **forget yer** sweet face."

To Thornton, Lee Waters said, gayly, "**when** shall we three meet again?" but when he took St. John's hand and held it closely pressed in **his**, he could speak no word; again and again he tried, but he could not command his voice. Till that moment he had not fully realized what that parting would be.

"Good by, Lee," said St. John, cheerfully, "we shall meet again, if not here — there " — pointing, as he spoke, to heaven; "God bless you."

A fortnight later, this telegram came to Mr. Grey from Washington: "Lee Waters died this morning, from hemorrhage of the lungs."

CHAPTER XXIII.

PROMOTION.

YES, it was too true. Lee Waters had passed through numberless perils and exposures, in camp and on the march; had fought as bravely as any, and more recklessly than most, at Manassas and Gettysburg, and had escaped death through all, and now, when it appeared to all human seeming that his health was far better than formerly, he had been suddenly taken down with a violent attack of bleeding at the lungs, which terminated his life in a few hours. He was in Washington at the time, whither he and Holdfast had been sent upon an errand by their superior officer. Mr. Grey, who had become much interested in Lee, and who knew that he had no friends out of the army to pay to his body the last tribute of respect, went immediately to Washington and brought back with him the mortal part of the young soldier. The funeral was attended from the house of a kind friend of Emily's, in the city, Mr. Grey and Thornton following to Greenwood as chief mourners. Poor Emily, it was a sad blow to her, and although she knew that there were thousands of hearts in the country suffering even as she suffered, it did not make her individual sorrow the less. But she did not mourn as one without hope, for the remembrance of the last few weeks of his life, his changed character and purposes, gave her the assurance that the change was for him a blessed one. For herself, life was full of duties which she would strive to perform faithfully, and, as she had strength, cheerfully.

Thornton felt Lee's loss as a personal grief. In spite of his faults he had become much attached to him in the army, and the weeks of companionship at home had drawn them still nearer together. Perhaps a few lines from Holdfast to Thornton may interest my readers.

DEAR SIR AND FRIEND: Hoping you'll 'scuse my poor writin', seein' 's I scursely ever take pen in hand, 'cept to Sally, who hasn't much larning herself, an' as I knowed you'd like to heer 'bout Lee, I'll tell you the little there is to tell.

Poor chap! we was both in high spirits when we come to Washington, for we knowed we was to have comissions, both on us, — he fust and I second lootenant. I never heerd him run on so wild like 'bout everything. He talked 'bout Miss Em'ly, said how much too good she was for him, and all that, and 'bout all yer good folks. He said nobody knowed how much good you done him by yer coorse in the army, and how often he felt 'shamed of his own ugly temper when you was so calm and cool like. He said one sich man's you was enough to salt a rigiment with savin' grace, or suthin' like it. And then he said, as for yer brother, he finished what ye begun, and altogether he owed ye both, and indeed all on ye, a heavy debt; but he'd try and square it off the way ye'd all like best. Then he'd sing and talk away, so full of fun and stories, and sich as I never heern before. Waall, I was n't with him when he was took; but when I come up to his room to look arter him, — we was going back that arternoon to camp, — I found him lyin' all white an' still on his bed, and a woman seein' to him. And then she telled me how he'd been bleeding, and how the doctor said he could n't git over it. Presently he opened his eyes, and said, "Good-by, old chap; no more fightin' for me here. Tell them, tell Emily — I am willing to go — and — give — my — love." Then he did n't say nothin' more for an hour or so, an' then he looked round sort of wild like, and said, "Don't run; we'll beat 'em yet; charge bayonets!" Then his look changed, an' he said, "Read in my Bible where the mark is;" an' he spoke so strong an' clear-like, I said, "He's getting better." She shook her head, an' I got his Bible, an' opened at the mark, an' there I found the chapter yer father read us that last night to yer house. I mean the one in the Old Testament. It was all marked, day of month an' all. I read it, an' he looked so bright an' pleased, an' after I got through he took my hand an' held it tight-like, as a little child might, an' then he seemed sinkin' an' sinkin' away, an' his lips jist moved, an' all I could make out was, "Though I walk through the valley," — an' then he stopped, an' never spoke agin, an' then — that's all —— Hoping ye 'r 'most smart agin, your sarvant an' friend,

JAKE BROWN.

St. John received the intelligence of Lee's death calmly, and said, "I did not think our separation would be so short. I cannot say poor Lee, I must say blessed Lee, for he would always have had a great deal to contend with, with his fiery temper and proud spirit, and religion does n't alter the whole temperament; it can't do that for us; it only helps us to control our passions. How glad I am I learned to know all the good there was in him, and how glad I was able to help him ever so little! Yes, he used to tell me how much good Thorny's example had done him."

Time passed on, and brought strength and healing on its wings to the elder, and weakness and decline to the younger brother; and Horace, with his buoyant spirits and exuberant life, looked with wondering awe and tender love upon the dear one who had never, in his wildest and rudest days, misjudged his heart.

Thornton was well, entirely well again. His wounds were all healed, his limbs had regained their elasticity and vigor, his full beard hid entirely the scar on his cheek, and he looked a man of twenty-five or thirty, so mature was his expression and bearing.

He reported his restored health to his colonel, at the same time asking for a little longer furlough on account of his brother's rapidly failing condition. He did not receive an immediate reply, and was hesitating whether to write again when the expected letter came.

It was the close of a beautiful autumn day. St. John lay upon a couch, propped up with pillows. He had never been confined to his bed for a day, and he had expressed the wish that he might not be. Just as Mr. Grey entered the library with Thornton's letter in his hand, Mrs. Grey had thrown back the blinds opening to the western sky, and a flood of golden light poured into the apartment. "See," said St. John, "the room is full of glory. A letter, — *the* letter for Thorny, father? A good omen for you."

Thornton took the letter, read it, his face flushing with pleasure, his eyes sparkling, handed it to his father, and said to St. John, "Yes, a good omen, a true one. I am promoted to a captaincy in my old company, to take poor Ned's place. It has been kept for me, only temporarily filled till now. Isn't it good news, Johnny, dear? Oh, what is the matter?" he exclaimed in a changed tone as he looked into his brother's face.

"Nothing bad, dear; perhaps I too am to be promoted. Call the others. I am glad for you dear, dear Thorny, and oh, so happy for myself! Mother, dear ones all, — good night, — *good* night."

This was all; with his mother's hand clasped in his, his father's laid lightly upon his brow, his pure spirit had passed on with his last words, "good night."

> "Good night! — now cometh gentle sleep,
> And tears that fall like gentle rain;
> **Good** night! O holy, blest, and deep,
> The rest that follows pain!
> How should we reach God's upper light,
> If life's long day had no 'good night.'"
>
> "Not dead, but born again,
> Born by a new celestial birth."

Henceforth the anniversary of that day shall be kept in Mr. Grey's family, not with fasting and mourning, though sad memories will mingle with bright hopes, but as a private Easter Sunday of their hearts. So far as practicable the family **will** meet together, and with reverent hearts and cheerful faces celebrate that celestial birthday. Pure, beautiful flowers shall decorate the rooms, and hymns of praise and thankfulness shall ascend to heaven.

After all was over, and love and reverence had

done all that could be done for the mortal remains of St. John Grey, the family sat together once more in the library, and talked in low voices of the dear one, not lost but gone before. Or rather Mr. Grey and Thornton talked, for Mrs. Grey sat back in her chair weary and sorrow-stricken, and Margaret on a stool at her feet laid her head upon her lap and pondered over the mystery of death, while Horace listened to his father and brother, but did not speak.

"How strange," said Thornton, "that my promotion and his summons came at the same time. I shall never, never, forget the expression of his face as he said, 'perhaps I too am to be promoted.' What earthly rank can equal his?"

"Yes," said Mr. Grey, "it was a beautiful thought. Death would lose its terrors if we could regard it in its true light; promotion from care and sorrow to peace and rest, from weariness of the flesh to full spiritual life, from the imperfect service of earth, to the perfect service of heaven."

"I shall attach a sacred significance henceforth to my promotion. I can hardly bear to think of scenes of blood and warfare after this sacred experience, and yet I must."

"We walk by faith and not by sight," said Mr. Grey; "war and the principles of Christianity are in direct opposition to each other, and yet my conviction never wavers that this is a God-appointed war, and that out of it we are to come purified and strengthened, and really worthy our great blessings and privileges. We shall all do our work of life better for the experience **of the** past few weeks, whether it be deeds of love and mercy, **or a** just resistance **to** wrong."

CHAPTER XXIV.

HORACE GAINS ANOTHER VICTORY.

"Are you going to the city this morning, Captain Grey?" said Horace, a day or two after the events I have narrated occurred.

"No, I think not, it is not necessary, and I don't feel much like it."

"Come with me then out into the woods, I want to talk to you."

"What is it," said Thornton after they had walked some distance; still Horace did not speak. "About your going into the army?"

"About my *not* going into the army, at least this autumn."

"Indeed, has the war fever left you then? If so, I am glad of it."

"On the contrary it is higher than ever. I never felt before so anxious to be in the army as I do now; but the long and short of it is, Thorn, that I can't make up my mind that it is quite right for me to go. If you don't understand why, I can't tell you."

"You're a brave fellow, Horace, braver than I am, after all. I *do* understand why. I ask your forgiveness for not seeing at once what you meant. I am so glad you have decided to stay at home. It would seem cruel to leave father and mother alone after all that has passed, though I know they would not think of themselves; but you are still so young they both dread to have you go. But how came you to think of it, Horace? I don't believe I should, in your place."

"Perhaps the first time I ever thought of it was the night before the boys went back to the army, and father said, if you remember, I might go with you if I wished it. This set me to thinking what could happen that I should not wish it. As soon as I understood what father meant, I felt bad enough, and it seemed as if I couldn't give up my plans; but I watched St. John, and saw how good and unselfish he was, even while he was so sick, and I knew what he would think it right to do in such a case."

"Did he, did Johnny ever say anything to you about this?"

"No, not a word. He never did talk much to me about being good, and all that. He understood me, St. John did, and always seemed to know just how I felt about things. He said once to me that I must take his place to father and mother, and that he was sure I would, for, — for I had a true, kind heart."

Here Horace stopped abruptly.

"Have you told father?" asked Thornton.

"No, not yet; I shall to-night. You see if I was older, I should feel that I ought to go with you at any rate; but now I suppose it's a clear case my duty is at home. Steve and Hal are going, and some other fellows I know in the city, but that's neither here nor there if it's right for me to stay at home."

"I said you were a brave fellow, and you are, Hor, — brave and strong to give up such a darling wish to a sense of duty, and, without a hint from any one either. Tell father, by all means; and if he thinks it right for you to stay at home, he will say so. Now let's have a good ride with Margaret; she looks pale, and the fresh air 'll do her good. I'll speak to her if you'll tell John to bring up the horses."

"Yes, — but, Thorny, I wish father wouldn't ask me *why* I've changed my mind. I don't want to talk about *that*."

"Well, perhaps he wont; I don't think he will, in fact."

Perhaps Thornton spoke to his father that evening before Horace saw him. At all events, when the latter said to him, "Father, if you please, I will stay at home this winter and enlist in the spring," he was silent for a few moments and then said, "Thank you, my boy, for this sacrifice of your feelings to your mother and myself. We could not consent to it, however, unless we felt sure that a delay would be better for you as well as ourselves. You shall help me in my counting-room and in my labors for the soldiers, and we shall have a busy and happy winter. So best shall we show our love for the dear one above."

"Oh, father, thank *you*. I am so glad you will let me help you. I don't want to study any more; I don't believe I *could* settle down to that. I don't think I was ever made for a scholar."

"Perhaps not for a distinguished one; **but you** *are* made for a true, faithful man in whatever you undertake. Believe me, my son, this sacrifice of your feelings to duty will be of more service to your character than you can foresee. Even I did not expect it of you. This is what I call controlling circumstances **to** your best good. If you can do it now you will do it hereafter. 'The boy is father of the man.'"

"I don't exactly **know** what you mean, father, about my controlling circumstances in this case. Haven't they controlled **me**?"

"Not exactly. If you had followed your wishes would you not have gone into the army this autumn, — were you not much more anxious to do so than ever before, partly because you felt sad and lonely, partly because your patriotism has increased with your knowledge of public affairs, and partly because it will be a broad field for **your** active and energetic nature?"

"Yes sir, that is true."

"Well, circumstances, then, would have urged your going into the army had you suffered them to control you, but you controlled them, you resisted their promptings, and the result will be as I have said, a lasting benefit to your character. You must not think, I repeat again, either your mother or myself would accept so great a sacrifice from you were we not persuaded it would be for your good."

And so it was decided, and no word passed between Horace and his mother upon the subject for weeks, although in her good-night kiss and fond pressure of his hand that evening he thought there was even more than usual tenderness.

He passed a busy and a happy winter, as his father had promised, and was more than repaid for the sacrifice he had made of his desires to a sense of duty, by the gratification that he saw his presence in the family gave to his parents and to Margaret.

Poor Margaret. St. John's death had been more of a loss to her than, in her innocent heart, she really was aware of, and after the excitement of an event so new and mysterious (for her parents had died before her remembrance) had passed off, she drooped and paled like a delicate flower touched with early frost. But here Horace came in to cheer and sustain her. He persuaded her to ride, drive, and walk with him; at first upon the plea of helping dispel his loneliness, and afterwards as a mutual pleasure and benefit. He enlisted her aid in little plans for assistance to the sick and wounded soldiers in the New York hospitals, and he enlivened her with his bright sallies and his abounding spirits.

In November, his father took Horace with him to the consecration of the National Cemetery at Gettysburg, which was a great delight to the ardent boy, not only for the new scenes it opened to him, but for the privilege he enjoyed of hearing the oration delivered upon that occasion by one of America's truest patriots and finest orators. Here, also, he met his brother, "Captain Grey," and had the gratification of seeing the estimation in which he was held by his companions in arms. Here, too, to his unbounded surprise, he met Van Dusen Whitmore, as second lieutenant in a Pennsylvania regiment. He was told that Van had **not** remained more than a few weeks in the school where his father had placed him, and that he had then **run away and enlisted as a private** in the company in which he now held a commission. He was very unpopular, however, with his men, being harsh and arrogant to them, and cruel and vindictive to the enemy. More than one dark story had already been told of barbarity to fallen and wounded foes, and those who had watched his **career** from **its** commencement in the army, prophesied disgrace or violent death. Horace also heard of Steve and Hal from one of **the officers of the regiment in** which they had enlisted. **Steve was spoken of highly for** his cool determination, and Hal for his bravery, amounting almost to rashness.

The winter has passed, and Horace is now viewing with great satisfaction and delight the preparations for his joining the army as a private in his brother's company. It is hard for him to keep within bounds his pleasure at the prospect before him; a pleasure enhanced by the knowledge that he has nobly earned the gratification of his long-cherished desires. I do not think such a broad-chested, tall, vigorous-looking youth, with so much resolution and energy expressed in his face, will remain a private very long. Those of you who have followed his course in these pages, can fancy for him as rapid promotion in the future as is reasonable to expect.

My story is finished. I will not slight your powers of penetration so much as to suppose you need to be told what its lessons are, but will simply express the wish that this book may prove something more to you than the recreation of an idle hour.

www.ingramcontent.com/pod-product-compliance
Lightning Source LLC
Chambersburg PA
CBHW032223230426
43666CB00033B/829